Speaking Vegetarian
The Globetrotter's Guide To Ordering Meatless in 197 Countries

by Bryan Geon

pilot books... *guides to the good life, all your life*

Copyright © 1999 by
PILOT BOOKS
127 Sterling Avenue
Greenport, New York 11944

Library of Congress Catalog Card Number: 98-8459

Library of Congress Cataloging in Publication Data

Geon, Bryan, 1970-
    Speaking Vegetarian: The Globetrotter's Guide to
    Ordering Meatless in 197 Countries by Bryan Geon
    p.   cm.
    Includes index

ISBN 0-87576-222-0 (alk. paper)

1. Vegetarian Cookery Dictionaries.
2. English Language Dictionaries Polyglot.
3. Vegetarian Cookery-Guidebooks.
4. Vegetarianism Guidebooks.

I.Title.
TX837.G395 1999
641.5'636 dc21   98-8459
                                                        CIP

*Printed in the
United States of America*

Bryan Geon, a long-time vegetarian and inveterate globetrotter, is no stranger to the difficulties of avoiding meat while traveling. He has visted over 50 countries and fended off such diverse offerings as antelope head in Mozambique, dried lizard-on-a-stick in China, roast guinea pig in Peru, and blood pudding in Britain. A graduate of Harvard University and the University of Michigan Law School, he lives in Portland, Oregon.

ACKNOWLEDGMENTS

The completion of this book would have been utterly impossible without the assistance of scores of individuals who gave selflessly of their knowledge and their time. Particular thanks are due to the following individuals:

Philippe Accilien, Razvan Adam, Ummul Ahmad, Ishfaq Ahmed, Lars Andersen, Mike Andrejka, Nyma Ardalan, Kagan Arik, Hatice Atkim, Marius Baciu, Chris Barbee, Boban Basic, Emil Beli, Jan-Tom Bellos, Burhan Belturan, Adolphe Bernotas, Samir Bhagwat, Peter Bjoern, Alison Brooks, Retha Calitz, Michael Charney, Niladri Chatterjee, Cheng-Yong Lee, Willard Chikavumba, Seng Chiu, Cory Clark, Katherine Cooper, Oliver Corff, Irma DeMaio, Baru Diakite, Rossen Dimitrov, Jone Dvauhimasi, Pavel Dvorak, EDUCA, Robyn Fass, Dennis Fiddle, Dana Foote, Jerry Frontosa, Terence Fu, Shakashe (Conrad) Gaopalelwe, Angela Gelli, Russ Gibbons, Vincenzo Giordano, Muhammad Hamid, Meghan Hays, Victor Herlianto, Michelle Higuchi, Alina Holgate, Nadeem Jamali, Vojin Janjic, Jianho Wang, Mahndra Joshi, Gillian Kahn, Sasho Kalajdzievski, Abdul Kamer, Byungsik Kang, Matoize Katsande, Tamás Kovács, John Kozyn, Christos Ktenas, Tatyana Kulyabina,

Michal Kurmanowicz, Victor Hugo Lane, Lesotho Cash Stores (Qacha's Nek), Daniela Lessa, Ales Lipuscek, Greg Liu, Josep Lopez Besora, Jack Lupic, José Machicao, Michael Martin, Yoko Masuzawa, Christy Mbonu, Sanath Meegalla, Francis Najarian, Samir Nassar, Eric Natanael, Tshimis Ngalamulume, Candide Nsabimbona, Jamie O'Connell, Hans-Henrik Ohlsen, William Omondi, Neven Orhanovic, Xavier Ormaetxea, Ana Osterman, Atul Paki, John Pandis, Hyun Ok Park, Mohammed Pasban, Patrick Patterson, Anne Paulin, Anna Pezacki, Homme Piest, Michael Piscopo, Fernand Poukie-Kono, Honoré Albert Rakotoarivony, Pierre-Michel Rameau, Gilbert Ramirez, Jr., Joe Reis, Cathy Relang, Markus Rieder, Pierre Rossi, Vincent Schonau, Fiona Scorgie, Uday Sekar, Mini Shambe, Asad Abu Shark, Ashok Shrestha, Cynthia Smith, Koobaï Souaïbou, Vladimir Stoyanovski, Daina Stukuls, John Subaykan, Anita Subramaniam, Pat Srinivas, Saurabh Thapliyal, Heang Tin, Todd Tocci, Svein Valfells, Peter Vanatko, Jacquelien Van Stekelenburg, Natasia Veikune, Kiril Vidimce, Zeenad Abdul Wahid, Kesang Wangdi, Andrea Williams-Stewart, N. Wongsurawat, Heidemarie Workman, Daniel Woubishet, Katy Youel, Muhammed Zaman, and Gayle Zilber, as well as to the many diplomats and other individuals who asked to remain anonymous. Extra-special thanks go to Karen Smith for her unflagging support and assistance.

CONTENTS

Speaking Vegetarian

INTRODUCTION

Dining is one of the great pleasures of travel. Besides its obvious function of simple nourishment, eating is a way to experience a country and its culture through its food. While upscale restaurants in major tourist destinations usually have menus in English, off-the-beaten-track or less expensive restaurants rarely do. Sometimes no menus are available in any language and in many countries people who speak English are equally scarce. It is always an adventure to order from a foreign-language menu and wait to see what mystery dish arrives at the table.

Unfortunately for vegetarians, in most countries that mystery dish is likely to contain meat. Most pocket phrasebooks do not address the problem and usually contain translations for quaint (but worthless to vegetarians) phrases like, "Are delicious traditional pork dumplings available in this establishment?" Those who choose not to eat meat are usually limited to four options: buy and prepare one's own food, avoid restaurants; eat meat if it comes; eat only dishes one can see in advance and hope no meat is hidden inside; stay home and miss the joys of travel.

The intent of this book is to make it possible for vegetarian travelers to communicate their particular dietary preferences virtually anywhere in the world. It is not intended to make you sound like a native speaker but when you speak in the language of the country you're visiting—even a few halting phrases—it is a sign of respect. This is bound to win you goodwill, even if your diet puzzles the person you address. Be aware, though, that the phrases contained in this book cannot solve every problem. Your wish for meatless dishes should get across, but some people will misunderstand the nature of vegetarianism or will consider you deprived and try to foist meat upon you for your own good. No phrasebook can overcome cultural and personality differences of this sort. You are on your own as a vegetarian diplomat.

While it is impossible to include every one of the thousands of human languages spoken throughout the world, the book contains phrases in the official or major languages for every country. The omission of minor languages should not be taken as a sign of cultural insensitivity, but rather as a concession to pragmatism to keep the book portable. You will find that most people speak a national tongue, at least as a second language, so even in cases where you cannot communicate directly to a local, someone nearby probably speaks the national language and will be able to translate for you.

The book does not adopt a single definition of "vegetarian". In most cases, it allows the reader to mix and match phrases to communicate exactly what one does or does not eat. Some people who consider themselves vegetarians only avoid red meat, while vegans avoid animal products entirely. Other travelers normally eat meat at home, but avoid it while traveling because of unsanitary conditions in some developing countries. This book is designed for all of these types of "vegetarians," and for everyone in between. A reference to fish, chicken, or cheese is not intended to offend strict vegetarians. (If the mere thought of someone eating any kind of flesh or dairy product truly offends you, there are, unfortunately, very few places in the world you can safely visit.)

The chapters are organized by region of the world, and subdivided by country; the Indexes contain page references for the languages and countries found in the book. Each country's section first offers a brief synopsis of the meatless entrees generally available there. While every common vegetarian dish is not listed, you'll get a good overview of what you can expect to encounter in a particular country. Remember that the availability of vegetarian food may vary significantly from one region to the next.

The second part of each country's section contains translations and phonetic pronunications of phrases a vegetarian can use when ordering food in the language of that country. And all listings contain a translation for the most important phrase of all: Thank you. Polite readers may note that many languages omit a translation for the word "please." This omission is intentional; a surprising number of languages do not have a word for "please" while in others it is reserved for extraordinary requests (such as a plea to spare one's life). Where the use of "please" is either impossible or inappropriate when ordering food, the sentences listed use the most polite phrasing possible.

In many parts of the world, vegetarians (as well as most locals) may be restricted to a diet that is heavy on starch and light on vegetables or fruit. This is a particular problem in certain developing countries in Africa, Asia, and Latin America. While on a short trip such a diet will probably not have a significant adverse effect on your health, if you plan to be gone for a substantial length of time, you might want to take vitamins or other nutritional supplements. It may also be a good idea to take along high-protein foods such as peanut butter or a supply of energy bars. Unfortunately, there really aren't many options that are both portable and nutritionally high in protein to bring so, to a large extent, in certain countries, vegetarians are restricted to a diet of starches and the like (hence my advice to bring vitamins).

Another unfortunate fact of life in some countries is that the very foods that are most attractive to many vegetarian travelers—salads, unpeeled fruit, and uncooked vegetables—can lead to serious health problems, or at least serious discomfort, if they are not

3

properly cleaned. These otherwise enticing items may harbor a variety of unpleasant beasties that will swiftly ruin your trip if eaten. So, unless you can be sure that the produce has been cleaned appropriately, it is better to eat only vegetables that have been thoroughly (and recently) cooked, and fruits that can be peeled.

While readers will find this book invaluable in restaurants, food stalls, or snack shacks, you might be presented with a dilemma that the book cannot solve. If you are a guest in a private home, you will discover that, in many countries, it is considered incredibly rude for a guest—even a polite, culturally sensitive vegetarian guest—to refuse proferred food. Especially in poorer households, your hosts may be insulted because they think you are patronizing them and trying to spare them the expense of buying meat or consider their offering to be beneath you. At the very least, eat as much as you can of any meatless food offered. You can try to pantomime that eating meat will make you sick (which it might) or that you are allergic. The danger is that a badly-done pantomime is likely to be even more insulting than leaving the food on the plate! Of course, you can simply eat the meat. That is a matter for your own conscience.

With that exception and this book as a tool, you should be able to get meatless food almost anywhere. While in some cases your diet may be limited to grains, starches, and legumes (in other words, the food of the poor in that country), you will also encounter delicious and unusual vegetarian dishes. Eat with pleasure, enjoy your travels (and don't forget to call the airline in advance of your departure to reserve a vegetarian meal)!

Phrases and Pronunciation

The phrases in this book have been standardized. Even though the literal meaning of a word or phrase in the original language may differ from the English words, the general meaning will be the same. For example, the sentence "I would like something without ___" might be best translated as "I want to eat a dish without ___ , please", or "I wish to eat food that does not contain ___."

The phrases and words have blanks in appropriate places so that you can mix and match words depending on what you specifically do or do not eat. ("I do not eat ___"; "I eat ___.") In some languages, the form of a noun like "meat" varies depending on how it is used; in these cases, the appropriate version of the word is the one directly below the sentence you are using.

The phrases are presented in a 3-column table. The first column displays a word or phrase in English. The second column features a translation of the word or phrase in the foreign language. (All foreign words are presented in the Roman alphabet.) Finally, the third column shows the phonetic pronunciation of the foreign words.

The phonetic pronunciations provided have been made as simple as possible within the bounds of reasonable accuracy. You are unlikely ever to be mistaken for a native speaker, and in some cases the pronunciation will sound awkward or unnatural, but you should be understood. The pronunciations should be read as if they were ordinary English words, and pronounced using standard English phonetics. Syllables in all capital letters should be STRESSED. A few important sounds are not self-evident, or have no obvious English equivalent. These are:

zh   'zh' denotes the sound of 's' in pleasure, or the 'zh' of Dr. Zhivago.

kh   the bold 'kh' is the guttural sound of German 'ch', or the 'ch' sound in the Scottish lo<u>ch</u>. When properly done, it sounds as if you are bringing up phlegm from the back of your throat.

ng   the bold 'ng' is pronounced as the middle 'ng' in si<u>ng</u>ing; the g is not strongly pronounced.

n   bold 'n' is not really an 'n' at all. This symbol is used to indicate that the preceding vowel sound is nasalized, as in French. (Try saying the vowel as if you were speaking through your nose.)

A few other sounds have more than one possible pronunciation

5

in English. The intended sounds for the purposes of this book are set out below:

g   'g' is always a hard sound, as in go, not the soft g of giant.

oh   'oh' is a long o sound, as in g<u>o</u>.

aw   'aw'   is always pronounced as in s<u>aw</u>.

ow   'ow' is pronounced like the exclamation of pain, or as in c<u>ow</u>.

uh   'uh' is a short u sound, as in n<u>u</u>t.

eye   'eye', or 'consonant-ye' combinations like 'dye' or 'rye', are pronounced as a long i, as in m<u>y</u>.

A Note on Tonal Languages

Many East Asian languages are tonal, so the meaning of a word can vary depending on the tone, or pitch, in which it is spoken. It is difficult to learn tones from a book (and not particularly easy to learn them from a live person). However, the closest analogy is to reading music—higher tones are at higher pitches, just like musical notes. In the pronunciations given in this book, three lines of text are used. The line on which the written translation occurs shows where middle pitch should be; words on the line above are high tones, words on the line below are low tones.

For example:

this one **high**

this is the **middle tone**

and this **low**.

There is no absolute standard of high and low tone; the pitches are relative to your ordinary way of speaking.

Individual words can also change pitch. Changing pitch is indicated by one of four symbols.

↗ This symbol shows that the word has a rising tone. A rising tone is said as if a question were being asked, or as if one were singing notes that were rising in pitch. This symbol is placed immediately in front of the phonetic pronunciation of the word.

↘ This symbol shows that the word has a falling tone. A falling tone is said as if one were emphasizing a word, or descending downwards in the musical scale. This symbol is placed immediately in front of the phonetic pronunciation of the word.

⌒ This symbol over a letter within the phonetic pronunciation of a word (e.g., â) indicates that the word rises in tone, then drops.

⌣ This symbol over a letter within the phonetic pronunciation of a word (e.g., ŏ) indicates that the tone falls, then rises.

Although proper pitch is important for comprehension, even if you botch things up superbly, you will probably still be understood in the context of the sentence. (You might also unintentionally cause guffaws among your listeners when you say something like, "I do not eat umbrellas." Don't worry about it; you're trying and that's what counts.)

chapter one
NORTH AMERICA:
ABROAD AT HOME

The United States and Canada have the most diverse populations in the world. Native speakers of every language in this book (and several hundred more besides) are found in both countries; the cuisines of a hundred nations are served in restaurants throughout the cities and countryside of North America. Even so, when most foreigners think of "American" food (or Canadian food, if they think of it at all), they are likely to think of quickie hamburgers or fried chicken. Fast-food franchises seem to be our contribution to world cuisine.

In reality, North American food is much more complicated and interesting. Every region has its local specialties, including a number of meatless delicacies—at the very least, desserts are usually vegetarian, if not vegan. Ethnic restaurants of every stripe are found in cities, and sometimes in the most unlikely rural areas: Chinese food in the Wyoming desert, Ethiopian food in small-town Michigan, Mexican food on the Saskatchewan prairie. Test the phrases in this book on restauranteurs who come from other countries (although you might not wish to try to impress your date at a fancy French restaurant). You'll find that, even while staying close to home, it is possible to travel abroad.

The United States

In the United States, most vegetarians—and consequently most specialist vegetarian or veggie-friendly restaurants—are concentrated in the cities of the Northeast and the West Coast. Resort areas and college towns across the country are also fertile ground. However, it is not difficult to get meatless meals anywhere in the country. Salad bars and all-you-can-eat buffets, while of wildly uneven quality, are common even in the solidly carnivorous Plains states. In small towns, restaurants are often happy to make grilled cheese sandwiches, or salads without chicken or bacon — although you may get a sidelong suspicious look if you state outright that you are a vegetarian.

Although **English** obviously predominates, the languages of every country on earth are spoken here, especially in the large metropolitan areas. Some languages are especially common in particular regions: Spanish is widely spoken in the Southwest and in Florida, as well as in the urban Northeast; French is used in parts of northern New England; German, Polish, and the Scandinavian languages form the linguistic heritage of many Midwesterners; Asian languages are common in urban areas on the West Coast; and in ethnic enclaves throughout the United States, people speak in the tongues and dialects of their native lands.

Canada

The vegetarian demography of Canada is much like that of the United States: urban areas in Ontario, Quebec and Western Canada have the heaviest concentrations of vegetarians (as they do of Canadians in general). Fish still figures heavily in the diet of Eastern Canada's maritime provinces, while the prairie provinces of Alberta, Saskatchewan, and Manitoba are hardly less carnivorous than their counterparts south of the border. Even so, meatless entrees can be found in restaurants almost anywhere in Canada—even in such unlikely locales as Whitehorse, the far-flung capital of the Yukon Territory.

Canada's linguistic picture is complicated by the sometimes uneasy coexistence of two official languages, **English** and **French** (p. 60). English is the native tongue of most Canadians. French is spoken in Quebec, and in scattered communities in other provinces. Although Montreal is largely bilingual, in other areas of Quebec English is not widely spoken and by law all signs must be in French. Thanks to a recent influx of immigrants, Cantonese and other East Asian languages are very common in Vancouver.

chapter two
LATIN AMERICA AND THE CARIBBEAN

L atin America and the Caribbean islands are the destinations most often visited by North Americans who travel abroad. Unfortunately, many of us know little about our neighbors to the south, and even less about their cuisines and languages. Most Americans and Canadians are familiar with so-called "Mexican" food, but the burritos and tacos at North American fast-food restaurants bear little resemblance to their cousins served south of the border. The many styles of Mexican cooking are in turn very different from the cuisines of nations further south or east.

Of course, there are some common elements to cooking in this part of the world. The staple meal in many Latin American and Caribbean countries is rice in combination with some form of beans—black beans, kidney beans, or pigeon peas. So far, so good. Unfortunately for vegetarians, the beans are often cooked in lard. In fact, lard is used in many fried foods, and is sometimes even added to butter. Furthermore, some apparently innocuous soups and stews contain bacon or ham for flavor.

The good news is that Latin America and the Caribbean feature a rich variety of regional cuisines and local dishes, not all of which rely on meat. Some dishes display the influence of immigrant groups, such as East Indians in the southeastern Caribbean or Italians in parts of South America. Other dishes work wonders with indigenous foods and local methods of cooking and spicery. Wherever you go, it is worth seeking out local dishes, even if you are ultimately forced to return to your old amigos, rice and beans. If you are searching for a change of dietary pace, remember that Chinese restaurants are found throughout Latin America and the Caribbean, and almost always serve vegetarian dishes.

There are literally hundreds of indigenous languages spoken in this area of the world. The vast majority of these languages have relatively few speakers; in other cases, a given language may have many dialects, each of which is spoken only in a small region. In most (but not all) cases, someone who speaks a country's primary or official language will be on hand if translation is required. For reasons of space, economy, and utility, this book reluctantly omits most of these languages.

Spanish dominates the hemisphere. Because it is used in almost 20 of the countries listed below, it is presented here first. There are some differences in pronunciation from one country to another, but the standard pronunciations below should be understood by Spanish speakers anywhere.

Spanish

Note: Throughout much of Spanish-speaking Latin America, the word for meat (*carne*) is typically understood to refer only to red meat, and sometimes only to beef, so you may need to be very specific about what you do or do not eat.

I would like something without ____.	Quisiera comer algo sin ____.	kee-see-YAIR-uh co-MAIR AHL-goh seen ____

Latin America and the Caribbean

We would like something without ____.	Quisieramos comer algo sin ____.	kee-see-YAIR-ah-mohs co-MAIR AHL-goh seen ____
I do not eat ____.	No como ____.	noh KOH-moh ____
I eat ____ and ____.	Como ____ y ____.	KOH-moh ____ ee ____
meat	carne	KAR-nay
chicken	pollo	POY-yoh
fish	pescado	peh-SKAH-doh
eggs	huevos	WAY-bohs
cheese	queso	KAY-soh
I am a vegetarian. (*male speaker*)	Soy vegetariano.	soy vay-hay-tah-ree-AH-noh
I am a vegetarian. (*female speaker*)	Soy vegetariana.	soy vay-hay-tah-ree-AH-nah
Please.	Por favor.	pohr fah-BOHR
Thank you.	Gracias.	GRAH-see-ahs

A. Mexico and Central America

Mexico and the Central American nations benefit or suffer, depending on your point of view, from the proximity of the United States. One side effect of the spillover of American culture is the proliferation of American fast-food establishments and chain restaurants in major cities throughout this part of the world. While the offerings will be (perhaps all too) familiar to you, a hamburger is unlikely to entice the average vegetarian. Fortunately, there is still a strong current of traditionalism, even in matters of cuisine. As elsewhere in Latin America, rice and beans are staple foods and are served with abandon (and you may indeed eventually wish to abandon them), but there are also national and regional specialties to be discovered—seek and you shall find.

Belize

While Belize has a remarkably cosmopolitan heritage, its cuisine, unfortunately, does not fully reflect this diversity. Excellent fresh seafood is available, but true vegetarians will find slim pickings. Vegetables are fairly uncommon and usually canned, although good tropical fruit is widely available (always peel or thoroughly wash in clean water). Rice, beans, and plantains (usually fried in lard, unfortunately) are standard fare. Some resorts and restaurants that cater to foreign tourists offer more variety, and generally have one or more options for vegetarians. If you crave Asian cuisine, there are Chinese and Indian restaurants in the larger towns; these may be the best options for vegetarians outside the resort areas.

English is the official language, but most people speak a Creole patois at home (although they generally can also speak standard English). Spanish (p. 14) is spoken in the north and west. Mayan languages, Garífuna (the language of the Black Caribs), and a German dialect (spoken by Mennonites) are also used in some areas of the country.

Costa Rica

Costa Ricans love meat but, luckily for vegetarian visitors, they also eat other foods from time to time. Pesco-vegetarians will be delighted, although probably not astonished, to learn that fresh seafood is available everywhere along the coasts. Restaurants featuring various European cuisines, as well as American fast-food standards, are scattered throughout the main cities. Pizza, pasta, and salads are particularly common, and there are Chinese restaurants everywhere. Bakeries serve up tasty meatless treats (but beware—some baked goods contain lard). Costa Rica also produces many varieties of cheese, so cheese sandwiches are an option for non-vegans. And of course, rice and beans can be found everywhere in the country.

Spanish (p. 14) is spoken throughout the country. English is spoken in some communities along the Caribbean coast.

El Salvador

The capital city, San Salvador, has a few specifically vegetarian restaurants, and a number of Italian and other European-style restaurants that serve some meatless dishes. Outside the city, as in rural areas throughout Central America, rice and beans are standard. *Pupusas*, tortillas stuffed with various ingredients and fried, are unique to El Salvador and are available throughout the country. While the fillings are usually beef, pork, or chicken, it is possible to find interesting meatless varieties that contain cheese, black beans, or pumpkin.

Spanish (p. 14) is the national language. A relatively small number of people, mainly in the highland areas, speak indigenous languages.

Guatemala

While relatively few Guatemalans are vegetarians, the constant stream of gringo vistors has resulted in the establishment of a number of vegetarian restaurants in Guatemala City and other well-touristed areas. Guatemala City also features an array of international cuisines (especially Italian restaurants serving pizza and pasta), with the usual sprinkling of Chinese resturants. In the countryside, rice, beans, eggs, and tortillas are the staples, often served with chicken. On the Caribbean coast, banana, coconut, and fried plaintains are commonly used. Fish-eaters will find that fresh fish is easily available on both coasts.

Spanish (p. 14) is the official language. Many Indians in the Guatemalan highlands speak an indigenous language as a native tongue, and some speak no Spanish at all (although someone who does speak Spanish is usually nearby).

Honduras

Both main cities (Tegucigalpa and San Pedro Sula) have a few vegetarian restaurants, as well as some restaurants that serve European-style food. The standard ensemble of rice, beans, and tortillas is found everywhere, in or out of the cities. Chicken is the most common accompaniment in inland areas; fish is usually served on the coast. Coconut is used extensively on the Caribbean coast, where it is used in making bread. There are Chinese restaurants in some smaller towns, as well as large cities. The Bay Islands in the Caribbean, off the north coast, receive large numbers of tourists, and many island restaurants serve meatless dishes.

Spanish (p. 14) is the national language. English is the first language of some communities along the north coast, and of most natives of the Bay Islands. Garífuna-speaking Black Caribs live in some coastal villages in the north.

Mexico

Contrary to the perceptions of many North Americans, Mexico has a highly varied regional cuisine (although, as in most Latin American countries, rice and beans are the staples almost everywhere). Indeed, the variety of Mexican cuisine can pose special problems for vegetarian travelers: furry jungle animals are consumed

18

in the Yucatán and the far south, and iguanas are sometimes eaten along the west coast. While pork, chicken, and beef are frequently used, there are many dishes that contain cheese instead of meat. Others feature wonderful salsas with vegetables and grains or potatoes. (Beware of lard, however). Fish eaters will be happy virtually anywhere along Mexico's thousands of miles of coast.

Vegetarianism has started to become something of a fad among the middle and upper classes, and there are a growing number of vegetarian restaurants in the cities and resort areas. Some restaurants in these areas also serve a variety of international dishes, including pizza and pasta. The standard array of American fast-food nightmares can be found in most regions of the country. Ever-useful Chinese restaurants are found in Mexican towns, sometimes in unlikely places such as the middle of the Sonoran Desert.

Spanish (p. 14) is the official language. There are also dozens of different Indian groups, each with its own language; some 20 languages are spoken in the Yucatán alone. Many Indians speak no Spanish, although someone who speaks Spanish can usually be found within hailing distance.

Nicaragua

The former Sandinista regime made a concerted effort to promote soya as an alternative source of protein. As a result, vegetarian restaurants serving soy dishes are scattered around Nicaragua, although they are not necessarily well-patronized. In rural areas, volunteer organizations use soya to reduce malnutrition (most locals, however, would still rather have meat). Despite the presence of soy, rice and beans are still the main foods for most Nicaraguans. American, Italian, and other European-style dishes are available in the cities. There are also Chinese restaurants in most Nicaraguan cities.

Spanish (p. 14) is the official language. English is the primary language in some villages along the east coast, while Indians in the remote, rural northeast speak indigenous tongues.

Panama

Panama sometimes bills itself as the crossroads of the world and since, unfortunately, the world seems to eat a lot of meat, so does Panama. As one might expect in a country with two seacoasts so close together, fish is also quite common, so pesco-vegetarians will be content. Tropical fruit is excellent and can be found everywhere. (It is always wisest to peel it first or wash thoroughly in purified water.) Traffic from the Panama Canal ensures the presence of a wide variety of international cuisines, including the expected Chinese restaurants, as well as the occasional exclusively vegetarian eatery. Despite the relatively cosmopolitan atmosphere here, rice and beans remain the staples for many people, especially outside the cities. In parts of the Darién jungle, it may be very difficult to find non-meat dishes and you might want to bring your own food e.g., high protein energy bars, peanut butter, etc.

Spanish (p. 14) is the national language. Due to the (rapidly dwindling) U.S. presence in the Canal Zone, many Panamanians speak English, and some English-speaking black Panamanians live on the Caribbean coast. Many Indians in the Darién speak indigenous languages and do not know Spanish.

B. The Caribbean

Rice and peas (pigeon peas or kidney beans) are the Caribbean staples—the island counterpart to mainland Latin America's rice and beans. The Caribbean islands have a diverse cultural heritage —in addition to the tourists that invade every winter from North America, immigrants have come from Africa, Europe, and Asia —and there is surprising variation in cooking styles within and between islands. Thanks to migrants from South Asia, on many of the English-speaking islands one can find *roti*, a thin pancake wrapped around a spicy filling. Usually *roti* is filled with meat, but some vegetarian varieties containing lentils or vegetables are available. As one might expect of islands, seafood figures heavily in

Caribbean cuisine. There are also plenty of unusual tropical fruits and vegetables to try. Unfortunately, on some islands local restaurants are difficult to find, and hotel and resort restaurants may offer the only sustenance. Such restaurants typically, but not always, offer at least one meatless dish.

Antigua and Barbuda

In local restaurants, there are peas and rice a-plenty. *Roti* and curries are common, if not always vegetarian, and West Indian-style seafood is found everywhere. In the hotel restaurants, "international" cuisine is the rule, and vegetarian entrees may not always be available.

English is the official language.

Bahamas

It is hardly surprising that in a nation made up of hundreds of islands, fish and shellfish feature heavily in the local cuisine. Conch in various forms is peddled everywhere, and boiled fish with grits (illustrating the contacts between the Bahamas and the American South) is a staple. For true vegetarians, options are few. Peas and rice are as common as they are elsewhere in the Caribbean, and peas are often made into a soup. Unfortunately, the soup usually contains meat for flavoring. The truly desperate vegetarian can ask local restaurants to prepare special meals, or can try tourist restaurants, which often serve pasta or pizza. Hotels usually offer salads or other light meatless dishes.

English is the official language. Many Bahamians speak a Creole dialect among themselves.

Barbados

Barbados offers limited vegetarian options, although fish-eaters will be happy. Flying fish is the national dish, and the island is strewn with British-style fish-and-chip joints. Curries are occasionally available, although they are not often vegetarian. *Roti* is available in some areas, and a diligent search can turn up interesting local specialties like pumpkin fritters, coconut pie, and cou-cou (okra and cornmeal). Otherwise, hotel and resort restaurants generally serve or can whip up some meatless dish.

English is spoken everywhere on this small island.

The British Islands

Anguilla is celebrated for its seafood (since its name means "eel," this may not be surprising). Shellfish is particularly renowned. Strict vegetarians will find that, unlike on some Caribbean islands, fresh vegetables are common here.

Bermuda, while not actually in the Caribbean, has Caribbean-style traditional cooking; rice and peas and fish dishes are found in local establishments. The tourist restaurants and resorts mainly serve "international" cuisine, with vegetarian dishes sometimes available.

In the **British Virgin Islands**, most restaurants are expensive, tourist-oriented establishments serving seafood and "international" cusine, and are not really geared toward vegetarians. Local food, which follows the typical Caribbean model, is usually not offered in restaurants.

On the **Cayman Islands**, traditional food is increasingly difficult to find, but it generally follows the standard Caribbean pattern. One variation is that sea turtles are raised for human consumption on Grand Cayman, so a heaping dish of endangered reptile is easy to get at local restaurants or in resort dining rooms. Such a dining experience is unlikely to interest vegetarians. Several of the resort hotel kitchens offer meatless entrees.

Montserrat once had some of the best fresh fruit and vegetables in the Caribbean. However, the volcano that devastated the island and caused the evacuation of most of the population has changed the food situation drastically. Visitors to Montserrat today are unlikely to find many vegetarian options, or indeed many food options of any kind.

The **Turks and Caicos Islands** are located just south of the Bahamas and have virtually identical food to that country. Seafood is king here.

These islands are British posessions. It should surprise no one that **English** is the language of choice.

Cuba

Cubans love pork, chicken, and seafood. However, thanks to Castro's policies and the economic effects of the U.S. embargo, most Cubans are currently unwilling vegetarians. Fresh vegetables generally are rare, although sweet potatoes and other root vegetables are relatively common. Fruit is often available. Unlike most Caribbean islanders, Cubans favor black beans over pigeon peas. Restaurants, limited in number and tightly regulated under the Communist regime, are slowly liberalizing, but some of the best food on the island is still only available in informal (and officially illegal) family-run restaurants.

Spanish (p. 14) is spoken throughout the country.

Dominica

Goat, chicken, pork, and seafood are all common. So is pond-food: giant frog legs (mountain chicken) is the national dish. Still, for those who eschew (rather than chew) amphibians, all is not lost. Some hotel restaurants offer vegetable platters, and there are a few vegetarian rastafarians on the island. Rice and peas are found here, like everywhere else in the Caribbean, and fresh fruit is both abundant and excellent.

English is the official language, but most islanders speak a French patois among themselves.

Dominican Republic

Santo Domingo has one or two vegetarian restaurants, but in general it is fairly difficult to get meatless food. Beef, pork, tripe, and goat, sometimes in the form of stew, are all standard, but rice and beans usually accompany the main dish and can, of course, be ordered separately. Some interesting vegetable pastries are available, and pizza and pasta can be found in towns. American-style chain restaurants are found in the cities, and have the advantage of offering safe-to-eat salads. In beach resort areas, hotels and restaurants sometimes offer vegetarian dishes. If you cook for yourself, you are likely to find that the quality of fruits and vegetables is generally higher in the Dominican Republic than elsewhere in the Caribbean. But wash carefully or peel as a precaution.

Spanish (p. 14) is the national language.

The French Islands
The French influence is obvious on these islands—patisseries, boulangeries, and crepe shops are found everywhere, and provide tasty meat-free carbohydrates.

Guadeloupe and **Martinique** have a vibrant Creole culture, and traditional Creole kitchens (which, unfortunately, emphasize meat and seafood dishes) are found alongside elegant bistros.

St. Barthélemy (often called St. Barts) and **St. Martin** have less of a Creole influence, and traditional European cuisine, particularly French cuisine, is prevalent in restaurants.

French (p. 60) is the official language. On Guadeloupe and Martinique, most islanders speak a Creole dialect among themselves. English is not commonly spoken.

Grenada
Grenada is famous for its nutmeg which, when consumed alone in large quantities, is mildly hallucinogenic and causes nausea. It is therefore wise to seek other sustenance. Meat and fish dishes are the focus, but vegetarian *roti* is sometimes available. There are also Italian restaurants that serve pizza and pasta. Of course, peas and rice are always an option, as is fabulous fresh fruit. Hotel restaurants present a final, and less than ideal, option; most have salads, but more substantial vegetarian dishes may not be on the menu.

English is the official language, but many islanders speak a French-African patois among themselves.

Haiti

Haiti is the poorest country in the Western Hemisphere so the average Haitian does not eat meat regularly. Rice with kidney beans and plaintains is the staple meal. Some interesting variations do exist, such as *riz djon-djon* (rice with black mushrooms). However, Haitians love meat when they can get it, so restaurants do not focus on meatless dishes. Fish is consumed along the coast, and there are a few French and Italian restaurants in Port-au-Prince (as well as a smattering of American fast food restaurants).

French (p. 60) is the official language. However, most Haitians cannot speak French, and **Haitian Creole** is the *lingua franca*. Even the educated upper classes speak Creole at home.

Haitian Creole

Because Haitian Creole is largely an oral language, the way it is used can vary significantly from one region to another. The phrases below are commonly-used constructions and, while not foolproof, should be understood in most parts of the country.

I would like something without _____.	Mwen vle manje san _____.	mwahn vlay mahnj sahn _____
We would like something without _____.	Nou vle manje san _____.	noo vlay mahnj san _____
I do not eat _____.	Mwen pa manje _____.	mwahn pah mahnj _____

25

I eat ____ and ____.	Mwen manje ____ ak ____.	mwahn mahnj ____ ehk ____
meat	vyann	vee-AHN
chicken	poul	pool
fish	pwason	PWAH-sohn
eggs	zé	zeh
cheese	fwomaj	fwoh-MAHJ
I am a vegetarian.	Mwen se vejetaryen.	mwahn seh veh-jeh-tahr-YEHN
Please.	Tanpri.	tahn-PREE
Thank you.	Mèsi.	MEH-see

Jamaica

Jamaica has a fair number of vegetarian Rastafarians and 7th Day Adventists so the concept of vegetarianism is not wholly alien. Indeed, there are a few vegetarian restaurants serving these clienteles. Unfortunately, outside these groups, vegetarianism is not widely practiced in Jamaica; goat and chicken are staples for almost all who can afford them or raise them on their own. Fish is widely available, however, which is good news for pesco-vegetarians; so is *roti* (which is good news for everyone else). Jamaica also produces a range of interesting and unusual fruits and vegetables such as breadfruit, ackee, and odd types of squash; it is sometimes possible to find these in dishes at local restaurants. In the resort areas, hotel restaurants and other restaurants that cater specifically to tourists are reasonably likely to offer meatless dishes.

English is the official langauge. Although the Jamaican patois is often difficult for outsiders to fathom, you will usually be understood perfectly.

The Netherlands Antilles

Aruba and **Bonaire** have excellent seafood and Indonesian restaurants (which sometimes have vegetarian options) are common on both islands. Curaçao, an oil refinery center, is more cosmopolitan and features a number of Latin American and European restaurants (as well as some delicious petroleum). Some of the European restaurants have meatless dishes. The cuisine of **St. Maarten** has a European focus, and if none of the options there appeal to you, you can easily cross to the French side of the island for a croissant.

Saba and **St. Eustatius** (Statia) offer more traditional Caribbean food. Peas and rice (sometimes cooked in stock) with meat or fish is the order of the day.

As one would expect, **Dutch** (p. 53) is the official language of the Netherlands Antilles. However, on the "ABC" islands of Aruba, Bonaire, and Curaçao, a Creole tongue called Papiamento is the everyday language of most islanders. On St. Eustatius, St. Maarten, and Saba, English is the first language of most islanders.

St. Kitts and Nevis

In addition to the inevitable rice and peas, shellfish and breadfruit are common food items here but few restaurants serve local food. Hotel and resort restaurants almost invariably offer "international" cuisine, which may or may not include meatless dishes.

English is the official language.

St. Lucia

In addition to standard Caribbean fare, visitors may encounter pumpkin soup, stuffed breadfruit, and flying fish (cooked, not air-borne). St. Lucia also produces wonderful tropical fruit in its lush rainforests. There are a few hotel restaurants and resorts which offer ordinary American or European dishes and ignore the local bounty.

English is the official language. Many islanders speak a French patois among themselves.

St. Vincent and the Grenadines
St. Vincent and the Grenadines (besides being a great potential name for a pop band) is composed of one big island and a string of small ones. Naturally, Vincentians eat a lot of seafood. All the Caribbean standards are available here; breadfruit is a local specialty, but is difficult to find in restaurants. Fresh local tropical fruit is excellent. Many of the resorts cater to the international yachting set, and do not concern themselves with vegetarians and other lower forms of life.

English is the official language. Many islanders speak a French patois among themselves.

Trinidad and Tobago
Many Trinidadians are of Indian (Asian, not Amerindian) descent, so vegetarianism is understood and accepted. Although Indian restaurants are surprisingly hard to find, meatless *roti* and curries are not. There is also a large Chinese community in Trinidad, with the inevitable accompaniment of Chinese restaurants. The Caribbean staples are found everywhere, except in tourist hotels, which tend to offer few vegetarian options. Trinidad's proximity to South America allows some Latin American influence to creep into the cooking.

English is the official language. Hindi (p. 191) is still spoken as a first language in many homes. Spanish (p. 14) is spoken in some districts.

The U.S. Islands
Puerto Rico is a culinary hybrid of Latin American heritage

and North American cultural imperialism. The staple diet is rice and black or red beans, served with seafood, red meat, tripe, or chicken. Puerto Ricans make delicious soups, but many of these have a bone thrown in for flavoring. Sometimes even rice is made with bones or bits of meat. One common meatless option is potato or other type of tuber prepared with olive oil. There are a few specialty vegetarian restaurants in and around San Juan. Puerto Rico also has many North American chain restaurants (including some with salad bars).

In the **U.S. Virgin Islands,** local cuisine is the standard Caribbean diet of rice and peas with meat or seafood. Most restaurants serve "international" cuisine and cater to tourists. Although tourist restaurants are not geared toward serving vegetarian dishes, salads, pasta, and pizza are usually available.

Since these islands are U.S. territories, **English** is widely spoken. However, in Puerto Rico the majority language is **Spanish** (p. 14). Virgin Islanders speak a lilting, Caribbean-accented English.

C. South America

South America has wonderfully varied climate and geography —from the glaciers of Tierra del Fuego to the Andean altiplano to the Amazon rainforest—so it stands to reason that South American cuisine varies correspondingly. While (as in Central America and the Caribbean) beans with rice or another starch serve as the basis of the diet for many people, there are other main dishes or accompaniments, and these differ dramatically from one country or region to another.

Demography also affects the type of food you will encounter. Countries with many immigrants or with a relatively large middle class, such as Argentina, Brazil, or Chile, have an international selection of foods distributed throughout the country. Poorer countries, such as Bolivia, offer fewer choices (and most choices that do exist are confined to cities).

Argentina

Argentinians consume more beef per capita than any other nationality. However, those who fear to visit this *non plus ultra* of carnivorousness should take heart; Argentina is not entirely off-limits. Buenos Aires has a burgeoning number of vegetarian restaurants (including some all-you-can-eat buffets), and in larger cities most restaurants have at least one meatless entree, generally of the salad/pizza/pasta genre. There are also many grocers who specialize in macrobiotic and vegetarian food; some serve prepared meals. Because of Argentina's long history of immigration, a variety of ethnic restaurants (particularly European restaurants) exist in most cities and large towns, and it is often possible to find meatless meals there, except in the most aggressively carnivorous areas.

Outside the cities, it is much harder to find meatless food, and vegetarianism is less tolerated. Cheese pizza and cheese and tomato sandwiches are relatively common almost everywhere, although an exclusive diet of these items might quickly grow tiresome. The one saving grace is that the traditional Argentine meal is centered around a single (usually huge) slab of beef so it is easy to eat around the meat. Fish-eaters will find that good seafood is usually available along the coast.

Spanish (p. 14) is the national language. There are also scattered immigrant communities which speak European or Asian languages, including German, Italian, Hebrew, and even Welsh. Some people along the Paraguayan border speak Guaraní (p. 37).

Note: Argentine Spanish is uniquely accented. One major difference from the pronunciations given at the beginning of this chapter is that pollo (chicken) is pronounced POY-zhoh, not POY-yoh.

Bolivia

In restaurants, Bolivian main dishes usually contain meat. Happily, although vegetarianism is by no means common, it is usually no problem to get meatless dishes if you ask for them.

Vegetable soup is common in the highlands. Bolivians on the whole are less inclined to argue about your dietary desires than some other nationalities. You are more likely to upset them if you refuse to drink beer. There are vegetarian restaurants in La Paz, Santa Cruz, Potosí, and other tourist centers. These cities also offer a variety of European-style food in cafes and restaurants.

The Bolivian countryside is a more difficult matter. In many poverty-stricken rural areas, people consider themselves lucky to even see meat and are bewildered if you do not share their joy at this treat. Remember though, the Incas genetically engineered the potato, and their descendants can serve you the miracle tuber today.

Spanish (p. 14) is the main language although Bolivia has a large population of Indians, many of whom speak no Spanish. Quechua (p. 38) is spoken in some highland regions. In the far south, Guaraní (p. 37) is spoken. In the Altiplano, **Aymará** is the language most commonly spoken outside the cities.

Aymará

Note that the Aymará word for meat, "aycha," signifies all types of flesh, not just beef. The term for beef is "huaca aycha"—cow meat. Sounds appetizing, doesn't it? Aymará dialects vary considerably, but the words and phrases below are fairly standard.

I do not eat ____.	Nayaja janiu man-queriti ____.	nye-AH-hah hah-NEE-oo mahn-kay-REE-tee ____
meat	aycha	EYE-shah
chicken	huallpa aycha	WYE-pah EYE-shah

fish	chalhua	SHAHL-wah
eggs	cauna	HOW-nah
cheese	quisu	KEE-soo
I am a vegetarian. *(Literally, "My food is what the earth produces.")*	Mancanaja yapu achuquihua.	mahn-kah-NAH-hah YAH-poo ah-shoo-KEE-wah

Brazil

Brazilian cooking varies significantly from region to region. Unfortunately for the vegetarian visitor, the cuisine relies on meat, and in rural Amazonia you may even encounter tapir, sloth, or armadillo on your plate if you aren't careful. Pesco-vegetarians will find that fish is available along the coast and near the Amazon, and spicy seafood dishes are a specialty of Bahia state. There are a few vegetarian restaurants in big cities like Rio and São Paulo, and restaurants in urban areas usually offer salads or pasta. Many ordinary restaurants are slowly beginning to add meatless entrees to their menus.

Thanks to the large number of immigrants and their descendants in Brazil, the cities also have European, Middle Eastern, and Chinese restaurants. São Paulo hosts a large Japanese population, so Japanese dishes are easily available there. Brazil has plenty of good fruit and fruit juices, bread, and cheese, so an impromptu picnic is always a possibility. And for better or for worse, the usual complement of American-style fast-food restaurants can be found in most urban areas.

Outside (and to a certain extent, inside) the cities, vegetarianism is considered terribly odd but acceptable; many Brazilians are de facto vegetarians living on beans and rice or manioc. Vegetarian travelers will have the greatest difficulties in southern Brazil, the home of friendly but militant red meat eaters. In this land of cowboys and *churrasco*—grilled beef—vegetarians are tolerated but certainly not catered to.

Portuguese is the official language. Spanish is similar enough to Portuguese to be understood, although Spanish-speakers will not understand the responses. French is probably the most common second language, although English is spoken in tourist centers.

Portuguese

I would like something without ____.	Eu gostaria de algo sem ____.	eyoh gohs-tah-REE-ah jee AHL-goh saym ____
We would like something without ____.	Nos gostariamos de algo sem ____.	nohs gohs-tah-ree-AH-mohs jee AHL-goh saym ___
We would like something without ____. *(colloquial version)*	A gente quer alguma coisa que não tenha ____.	ah JEN-chee kehr ahl-GOO-mah KOY-zah kay now TAYN-yah ____
I do not eat ____.	Eu não como ____.	eyoh now KOH-moh ____
I eat ____ and ____.	Eu como ____ e ____.	eyoh KOH-moh ____ ee ____
meat	carne	KAHR-nee

chicken	galinha	gah-LEEN-yah
fish	peixe	PAY-shay
eggs	ovos	AW-vohs
cheese	queijo	KAY-zhoo
I am a vegetarian. *(male speaker)*	Eu sou vegetariano.	eyoh soh vay-zhay-tah-ree-AH-noh
I am a vegetarian. *(female speaker)*	Eu sou vegetariana.	eyoh soh vay-zhay-tah-ree-AH-nah
Please.	Por favor.	pohr fah-VOHR
Thank you. *(male speaker)*	Obrigado.	oh-bree-GAH-doh
Thank you. *(female speaker)*	Obrigada.	oh-bree-GAH-dah

Chile

Unlike neighboring Argentina, where meat is served separately in a large hunk, main dishes in Chile often consist of bits of meat mixed in with the other ingredients in your meal. Naturally, this presents a problem for vegetarian diners. There are a few vegetarian restaurants in Santiago, and meatless pasta dishes or salads are usually available in urban restaurants. Pizza is a reasonably common snack item. Assorted European and other international cuisines are well-represented in the larger cities and in touristed areas such as ski resorts or wine regions; these restaurants often offer at least one meatless entree.

Outside the cities, people may regard vegetarians as deprived and think they are doing vegetarians a favor by giving them meat. With concerted effort, a feigned allergy or other medical problem, you should be able to have your way. Fish-eaters will have an easier time, as seafood is available everywhere; eel, as a matter of fact, is the national dish.

Spanish (p. 14) is the national language. Some Aymará (p. 31) is spoken in the far northeast. A few scattered immigrant communities speak Italian or German.

Colombia

Vegetarianism is considered very strange in most of this country, especially the interior. However, it has become more acceptable in recent years and a few vegetarian restaurants have opened in the cities. There are European and Asian restaurants in the cities and you can usually find pasta, pizza, or some other viable meatless alternative for sustenance. Colombia's cuisine is highly regional, but unfortunately the regions all use lots of meat; guinea pig is considered a delicacy in the southern interior. Rice and beans are usually available (but beware of lard), and yogurt is plentiful.

Spanish (p. 14) is the official language. A few communities in the Andes speak indigenous languages.

Ecuador

Ecuador, like Columbia, is a country where vegetarianism is an oddity. However, in Quito and Cuenca it is fairly easy to find vegetarian restaurants, usually run by foreigners. Tourist-oriented restaurants, while not specifically vegetarian, routinely offer meatless dishes. Soy milk and tofu are available in cities. The cities also have a fair variety of Italian, Asian, or (heaven help us)

American-style restaurants. In smaller towns, restaurants will usually prepare your meal without meat if you ask. Yogurt is very popular throughout the country, and many soups, especially in the highlands, are meatless. Bars often serve meatless side dishes; just be prepared to answer a few pointed questions if you don't drink beer.

Spanish (p. 14) is the official language. Many Indians speak indigenous languages; the most common of these is Quechua (p. 38).

French Guiana

Beans and rice or tubers, served with meat or fish, is the typical meal here but bakeries, *creperies*, and French restaurants, found throughout the country, generally offer something meatless to eat. There are also Vietnamese and East Indian restaurants serving meatless dishes. French Guiana is home to cayenne pepper, so it should shock no one that Guianese food is often spicy.

French (p. 60) (surprise!) is the official language of French Guiana. Some Asian immigrant groups speak their native languages, and a few Amerindians in the interior speak indigenous tongues.

Guyana

Because Guyana has many citizens of East Indian descent, vegetarianism is generally accepted and understood. The population here is a polyglot of races and cultures—African, Creole, Native American, Asian, Portuguese and English—and the country's cuisine reflects this diversity. Unfortunately, most of these otherwise diverse dishes have one thing in common; they contain meat. Seafood, usually with rice, is very easy to find. Curries and *roti* are often available in meatless form, and salted roast chickpeas are sold as a snack on the street. A major plus for vegetarians in Guyana is that most pastries contain vegetable shortening instead of lard.

English is the official language. Most Guyanese speak a Creole dialect in addition to standard English. Amerindian languages,

Hindi (p. 191), and other Asian languages are spoken in some areas.

Paraguay

Although Paraguayans seem to accept vegetarianism, it is far from common. While meat is standard in the Paraguayan diet, many dishes contain only cheese. *Sopa Paraguayana*, a kind of soufflé, is often made without meat. Pasta, rice, and vegetables are usually available as side dishes in restaurants, and Asunción has European and American-style restaurants which occasionally have acceptable meatless dishes.

The official languages are **Spanish** (p. 14) and **Guaraní**. Most Paraguayans are bilingual, but Guaraní is usually spoken by preference outside Asunción.

Guaraní

I do not eat ____.	Che ndakarúi ____.	sheh ndah-kah-ROO-ee ____
I eat ____ and ____.	Che akaru ____ ha ____.	sheh ah-kah-ROO ____ hah ____
meat	so'o	soh-oh
chicken	ryguasu	rih-wah-SOO
fish *(also means "skin")*	pire	peer-deh
eggs *(literally, "hen's eggs")*	ryguasu lupi'a	rih-wah-SOO loo-pee-UH

cheese	kesu	kay-SOO
Thank you.	Aguije ndeve.	ah-wee-JEH ndeh-veh

Peru

The national dish of Peru is *cuy*, or guinea pig (which, fortunately, is not often on the menu of tourist-oriented restaurants). Although vegetarianism is not widely practiced, those who do not want their dinner plucked from a Habitrail™ do have a few options. Italian, Asian, and other cuisines (as well as American fast-food restaurants, alas) are found in the cities, and there are even a few specialty vegetarian restaurants. The supermarkets in the cities stock tofu and soy milk. In tourist centers such as Lima and Cuzco, enterprising foreigners have opened vegetarian-friendly restaurants that cater mostly to North American and European travelers. Outside these areas, or if the expatriate scene is not your cup of coca tea, you can ask restaurants to prepare a special meatless meal. Potatoes are consumed everywhere (sometimes with meat, however). There are also many Chinese restaurants (called *chifas*), even in fairly small towns.

Spanish (p. 14) is spoken in most of the country. Aymará (p. 31) is spoken in some parts of the Andes, as is **Quechua**. There are many local indigenous languages spoken in the eastern jungle. Over two million Amerindians in Peru speak no Spanish whatsoever.

Quechua

With over 30 dialects spread among 6-10 million speakers throughout the Andean countries, there is no such creature as "standard" Quechua. The few phrases listed below are from a common Peruvian dialect, and should be at least partly understood by most Quechua speakers.

I do not eat any kind of meat.	Mana ima laya aychata mikunichu.	MAH-nah EE-mah LAH-yah eye-CHAH-tah mee-koo-NEE-choo
Please.	Allichu.	ah-YEE-choo
Thank you.	Yusulpayki.	yoo-sool-PAY-kee

Suriname

Thanks to Suriname's large population of Indians and Indonesians, meatless dishes are available in most areas of the country. The vast majority of the population lives along the coast, and seafood, usually served with rice, is a staple.

Dutch (p. 53) is the official language, although a native dialect called Sranan Tonga is the everyday langauge of most Surinamese. Standard English is widely spoken. Hindi (p. 191) and Javanese (p. 228) are spoken among the Asian community.

Uruguay

Uruguayans tend to brag about the high quality of their beef, and their meat intake is nearly as high as that of their Argentine neighbors. However, cholesterol consciousness is taking hold and vegetarian food is not too difficult to find. Montevideo has several vegetarian restaurants and a surprising number of macrobiotic food stores, many of which sell prepared meals to eat in the store (at tables) or to take away. Coastal resorts offer a nice selection of restaurants that serve some meatless dishes. The cities also have a good variety of European-type restaurants which usually serve a meatless dish or two. Even outside Montevideo, most restaurants offer at least one meatless entree (usually centered around pasta or salad).

Spanish (p. 14) is spoken throughout the country. Some localized immigrant groups speak other European langauges.

Venezuela

In Caracas, vegetarianism has become fashionable in some quarters over the last few years (partly because of the high cost of beef), so it is fairly easy to go meatless. Zona Las Mercedes has a concentration of vegetarian restaurants, and there are many ethnic restaurants (Indian, Middle Eastern, Italian) throughout the city where it is possible to get meatless food. Outside Caracas, however, vegetarianism is much less common, and many rural people consider it an extremely strange custom that leads to thin blood and weakness. Even apparently meatless dishes often contain bits of bacon or pork. The best option in rural areas probably is to create meals from side orders, and make your dietary desires clear.

Spanish (p. 14) is the official language.

chapter three
EUROPE

To many North Americans, European food is the most immediately familiar foreign cuisine. Of course, there is no such beast as "typical" European food; depending on ethnic background and a host of other factors, a person describing European food might be thinking of anything from pasta to fish and chips to borscht to escargot.

Although much European food appears immediately familiar to a visitor, Europe is a polyglot of cultures and cuisines and in almost every country in Europe there are many regional and local dishes that will be utterly unfamiliar. Some of these dishes will be meat-free while others will contain meat (and some may be vaguely frightening regardless of their meat content). It is therefore impossible to generalize with any degree of usefulness about the availability of meatless food—except to say that vegetarianism is most common in northern Europe, least accepted in eastern Europe, and generally easier to practice in cities than in rural areas. With perseverance, you should be able to find something meatless to keep you alive anywhere, and with luck that something will actually be nutritious and tasty.

The countries in this section have been divided, based on loose linguistic, cultural, and geographic affinities, into three sections: Northern Europe, Southern Europe, and Eastern Europe.

A. Northern Europe

The cuisines of Northern European countries traditionally centered on meat or fish. These carnivorous habits resulted partly from geography and climate, partly from the relative affluence of these countries. However, especially in the last 20 years, this affluence, combined with increasing health-consciousness and ecological sensibility, has resulted in a growing concentration of vegetarians in this part of the world. There are substantial numbers of vegetarians (and vegetarian organizations) here, and the upshot is that Northern Europe is one of the easiest places in the world for vegetarian travel. In most (but not all) northern countries, it is reasonably easy to find vegetarian or whole-food restaurants or meatless meals on the menus of ordinary restaurants. As elsewhere in the developed world, however, the range of vegetarian options is better in large towns and cities than in rural areas.

Austria

While Austrian food is traditionally very heavy and meat-oriented (think *wiener schnitzel*), the situation for vegetarians is improving. Most larger Austrian towns have one or two vegetarian restaurants; Vienna has several, including some exclusively vegan establishments. Many ordinary restaurants, especially in cities and resort areas, offer at least one vegetarian entree. There are also a fair number of ethnic restaurants (particularly Indian, Middle Eastern, and Asian) where vegetarian meals may be enjoyed. Non-vegans can subsist if necessary on Austrian dairy products, which are uniformly excellent.

German (p. 47) is the principal language in Austria. English is a common second language.

Belgium

Classic Belgian cuisine is widely acclaimed but vegetarians might not feel so enthusiastic because Belgians tend to use lots of meat. (Belgian chocolate, thankfully, tends to be meat-free.) Most larger towns, however, have at least one vegetarian restaurant and Brussels has a wide variety of vegetarian restaurants. Ordinary Belgian restaurants are beginning to offer meatless meals, or at least entree salads. There is also an abundance of Asian restaurants and Middle Eastern fast-food establishments, almost all of which serve some vegetarian food. While they are unlikely to provide the staple of your diet, waffle stands can be found everywhere.

Flemish and **French** (p. 60) are the national languages. Generally, French is spoken in the south of the country, while Flemish is spoken in the north. Brussels is officially bilingual. Although there are some minor differences in dialect, Flemish is essentially the same language as **Dutch** (p. 53).

Denmark

Vegetarianism is quite common in Denmark, and just about every restaurant in Copenhagen and other cities and large towns has one or more meatless dishes on the menu. There are also some veggie-friendly ethnic restaurants, as well as a number of exclusively vegetarian restaurants. In the smaller towns of Jutland, it may sometimes be difficult to get vegetarian entrees and you may be forced, occasionally, to make due with potatoes and boiled vegetables. If you can find a good traditional breakfast, which usually features cereal, fruit, and cheese (as well as meat and fish), you might be sated until dinner. Most fast-food in Denmark is meat-based, but the common smørrebrød—traditional open-faced sandwiches—are sometimes made with cheese or vegetables.

Speaking Vegetarian

Danish is the national language. English is widely spoken as a second language.

Danish

English	Danish	Pronunciation
I would like something without _____.	Jeg vil gerne have noget uden ___.	yai vihll GAIR-nuhr HAY noh-weht OO-then ____
We would like something without _____.	Vi vil gerne have noget uden ____.	vee vihll GAIR-nuhr HAY noh-weht OO-then ____
I do not eat _____.	Jeg spiser ikke ___.	yai SPEE-zuhr ICK-kuh ___
I eat _____ and _____.	Jeg spiser ___ og ___.	yai SPEE-zuhr ___ oh ___
meat	kød	koo-uhd
chicken	kylling	kyoo-ling
fish	fisk	fihsk
eggs	æg	ehg
cheese	ost	oost
I am a vegetarian.	Jeg er vegetar.	yai air VEEG-eh-tahr
Thank you.	Tak.	tahkk

44

The largely self-governing **Faeroe Islands**, awash in the frigid North Atlantic, are not exactly a haven for vegetarians. The main foods are fish, dried mutton and other meat (including the occasional beached whale) served with potatoes; fresh vegetables are scarce. The people speak Faeroese, an ancient Scandinavian tongue that is similar to Icelandic (p. 50). Danish is usually spoken as a second language.

Greenland (Kalaallit Nunaat), despite the promising name, is one of the least congenial spots on earth for non-fish-eating vegetarians (fish eaters should be fine). Most green growing things must be imported, and are extraordinarily expensive, when available. Most Greenlanders learn Danish in school; their native language, Greenlandic, is an Inuit (Eskimo) tongue.

Finland

Vegetarianism is not wholly unheard of in Finland, but it is not as common as it is in Denmark or Sweden. In Finnish cities, one can usually find at least one meatless entree on most menus. There are a good number of vegetarian and veggie-friendly restaurants in Helsinki. Fish eaters will be happy anywhere, but outside the cities strict vegetarian options are scarce. Beware of well-intentioned Finns encouraging you to eat the local game, such as Donner, Blitzen, and their brethren reindeer. If you can find them, there are some good traditional meatless soups, including cold fruit soup. A last (or first) resort might be one of the pizzerias that are found in towns throughout Finland.

Finnish is the national language. Swedish (p. 56) is also widely spoken, especially in the west. English is a common second language in and near the larger cities.

Finnish

I would like something without _____.	Haluaisin jotakin ilman _____.	HAH-loo-eye-sihn YAW-tah-kihn EEL-mahn _____

We would like something without ____.	Haluaisimme jotakin ilman ____.	HAH-loo-eye-sihm-meh YAW-tah-kihn EEL-mahn ____
I do not eat ____.	En syö ____.	ehn syoo ____
I eat ____ and ____.	Syön ____ ja ____.	SYOO-ehn ____ yah ____
meat	lihaa	LIH-hah
chicken	kanaa	KAH-nah
fish	kalaa	KAH-lah
eggs	munaa	MOO-nah
cheese	juusto	YOOS-taw
I am a vegetarian.	Olen kasvissyöjä.	AW-lehn KAHSS-viss-yoo-yah
Thank you.	Kiitos.	KEE-tawss

Germany

Traditional German cooking is heavy on red meat, particularly pork and what might be euphemistically called pork products. However, Germany—if you'll pardon the pun—is by no means the *wurst* country in the world for vegetarians. In western Germany, vegetarianism is quite common and there are even significant numbers of vegans. Most cities and large towns have vegetarian or natural food restaurants, and many more mainstream restaurants offer one or more meatless dishes. At the very least, you should be able to get salad and pasta or pizza. There are also many ethnic restaurants, especially Middle Eastern and Indian, serving up vegetarian salvation. Acceptable snacks are relatively abundant: potato pancakes are common, as are other potato products such as potato salad (spicier than the American version) and fries. For picnics or self-made snacks, German bread and cheese are cheap, tasty, and filling.

In formerly communist eastern Germany (apart from Berlin), vegetarianism has not yet established itself, and it may be difficult to avoid meat. While the concept of vegetarianism is slowly seeping eastward, many restaurants still serve only meat or fish entrees. A few vegetarian restaurants have opened in the cities, but creativity may be called for elsewhere. For the next few years, standard German side dishes such as sauerkraut and assorted potato concoctions may have to suffice.

German, with regional differences in dialect and pronunciation, is spoken throughout the country. English is a common second language, especially in the west.

German

I would like something without ____.	Ich hätte gerne etwas ohne ____.	ikh HEH-teh GAIR-neh EHT-vahss OH-neh ____
We would like something without ____.	Wir hätten gerne etwas ohne ____.	veer HEH-tehn GAIR-neh EHT-vahss OH-neh ____
I do not eat ____.	Ich esse kein____.	ikh EH-seh kyne ____

47

I eat _____ and _____.	Ich esse _____ und _____.	ikh EH-seh _____ oont _____
meat	fleisch	flysh
chicken	huhn	hoon
fish	fisch	fish
eggs	eier	EYE-uhr
cheese	käse	KAY-zeh
I am a vegetarian. *(female speaker)*	Ich bin vegetarierin.	ikh bihn feh-geh-TAH-ree-ehr-een
I am a vegetarian. *(male speaker)*	Ich bin vegetarier.	ikh binn feh-geh-TAH-reer
Please.	Bitte.	BIH-tuh
Thank you.	Danke.	DAHN-kuh

Great Britain

Great Britain is the home of such vegetarian nightmares as roast beef, steak and kidney pie, and haggis. Britain, on the other hand, also happens to be the home of one of the largest groups of vegetarians in Europe. (This is somewhat ironic, considering that meat is one of the few things the British historically have been able to cook well. Fortunately, the overall quality of British restaurants has improved significantly in recent years.) Nevertheless, there are vegetarian or wholefood restaurants in most large and many small towns throughout Britain. The majority of restaurants and a large number of pubs now offer vegetarian entrees. There are even vegetarian resorts and bed and breakfast hotels scattered around the country. As an extra safeguard for worried vegetarians, Britain's status as former imperial power means that restaurants representing cuisines from all corners of the world can be found in Britain. Indian restaurants and take-aways are particularly common, and can be found even in fairly small towns.

The rosy picture—painted above—of a veggie-friendly Britain must now be put into perspective. British fast-food, like American fast-food, is meat-oriented and in very small towns, especially in rural Wales, Scotland, Northern Ireland, and the north of England, it may be difficult to find a meal without meat. Lard is still commonly used for frying. And even in the cities, many restaurants do not serve meatless entrees (although even some steakhouses have vegetarian plates). However, all things considered, it is relatively easy for a vegetarian to keep well-fed in Britain.

While the accent in some regions may *sound* like a foreign language, **English** is the main language of Great Britain and English-speaking visitors should have few problems being understood. A few people in the far west and north speak Welsh or Gaelic as a first language.

Iceland

Unlike its mainland Scandinavian cousins, Iceland is not a very nice place for vegetarians. At last count there was one vegetarian restaurant in Reykjavík; the situation is otherwise fairly bleak. Icelanders eat what they can produce on or around their none-too-fertile island—in other words, fish, sheep, and poultry or sea birds. People who resolutely refuse to eat fish will probably be driven to cooking for themselves, or living off side dishes at restaurants. Vegans may slowly starve. As some compensation, Icelandic bread is good and cheese and yogurt are widespead and tasty.

The national language is **Icelandic,** an archaic descendant of Old Norse. Many Icelanders speak excellent English.

Icelandic

I would like something without _____**.**	Gæti ég fengið eitthvað ekki með ____.	gye-tih yehgg fehn-gith ayte-vahth ehk-kee mehth ____
We would like something without _____**.**	Gætum við fengið eitthvað ekki með ____.	gye-turm vith fehn-gith ayte-vahth ehk-kee mehth ____
meat	kjöti	KYUHR-tay
chicken	kjúklingi	kyook-leen-gay
fish	fiski	fihss-kee
eggs	eggjum	ehg-yurm
cheese	osti	ohss-tee
I do not eat _____**.**	Ég borða ekki ____.	yehg BOHR-thaw ehk-kee ____
I eat _____ **and** _____**.**	Ég borða ____ og ____.	yehg BOHR-thaw ____ ohrg ____
meat	kjöt	kyuhrt
chicken	kjúkling	kyook-lihng

fish	fisk	fihsk
eggs	egg	ehg
cheese	ost	ohsst
I am a vegetarian.	Ég er grænmetisæta.	yehg ehr gryne-meh-tihss-EYE-tah
Thank you.	Takk.	tahk

Ireland

Some say that a person stranded on a desert island could survive on Guinness alone. Presumably, however, most of us require additional sustenance and vegetarians will find Ireland—while no culinary paradise—to be a country where it is relatively easy to get meatless meals. There are vegetarian restaurants (although relatively few and far between) and more and more mainstream restaurants are beginning to add meatless entrees to their menus. There are also various ethnic restaurants, particularly in Dublin, as well as the standard collection of pizza and pasta places. Off the beaten path, however, it remains difficult to avoid lamb which may appear in any number of guises, especially Irish stew. Fish eaters will have little problem, even in the countryside, but others may have to survive on carbohydrates alone: potatoes are abundant (the famine having ended a century and a half ago), and Irish breads are some of the most unique and delicious in the world. Seaweed is harvested and eaten as a regular food.

English is spoken almost everywhere. A few communities, mainly on the west coast, speak Gaelic as a first language, but almost everyone understands English.

Luxembourg

Luxembourg is so small that it cannot really be said to have a distinctive cuisine of its own. The food generally features lots of meat, and is similar to traditional German or Belgian cooking. A good percentage of restaurants serve vegetarian dishes (especially pasta or salads), but one cannot expect great variety and creativity in Luxembourgish meatless offerings.

French (p. 60), **German** (p. 47), and Letzeburgesch (a Germanic dialect) are the official langauges. English and other European languages are spoken by many residents, especially in the capital.

Netherlands

Although traditional Dutch cuisine is meat-and-potatoes oriented, the Netherlands is one of the easiest European countries in which to be vegetarian. There are many specialized vegetarian restaurants in the cities and towns, and most general restaurants have at least one or two vegetarian options on the menu; sometimes they have a rather extensive selection. The cities, particularly Amsterdam and Rotterdam, offer an impressive array of often-meatless ethnic food: Indonesian; Surinamese; and Middle Eastern food are most common. Non-vegans are in for quite a good time in the Netherlands—anyone who loves cheese and does not find happiness in Holland may wish to seek professional help. Dutch bread is also excellent, and whole grain varieties are commonplace. However, Dutch snacks and fast-food still tend to focus on meat. In addition, meatless dishes may be harder to find (although they do exist) in small towns, especially in the south and east.

Dutch is the official language. Many people in the Netherlands speak English almost as well as you do, and may cringe at your attempts to speak their difficult native language.

Dutch

I would like something without ____.	Ik vil graag iets zonder ____.	ihk fihl **khrahkh** eets SOHN-duhr ____
We would like something without ____.	Wij villen graag iets zonder ____.	vay FIHL-lehn **khrahkh** eets SOHN-duhr ____
I do not eat ____.	Ik eet geen ____.	ihk ayte **khayn** ____
I eat ____ and ____.	Ik eet ____ en ____.	ihk ayte ____ ehn ____
meat	vlees	flayss
chicken	kip	kihp
fish	vis	fihss
eggs	eieren	EYE-yuh-rehn
cheese	kaas	kahs
I am a vegetarian.	Ik ben vegetariër.	ihk behn FEH-khuh-TAH-ree-uhr
Please. *(to elders and others you wish to address respectfully)*	Alstublieft.	ahls-TOO-bleeft

53

Please. *(to people in the same social class)*	Alsjeblieft.	ahls-YUH-bleeft
Thank you. *(respectful)*	Dank u wel.	dahn koo vehl
Thank you. *(to people in the same social class)*	Dankje wel.	dahn-KYUH vehl

---

Norway

It is not an easy or enviable task to be a vegetarian in Norway but the concept is gradually becoming more acceptable, especially among younger people. Oslo has a few vegetarian restaurants, and the city's ordinary restaurants are slowly incorporating meatless dishes into their menus. Outside Oslo, however, it remains difficult to find good vegetarian meals and along the northern coastline, it is almost impossible. Since Norwegians have traditionally eaten fish virtually by the boatload, pesco-vegetarians are in an excellent position. Stricter vegetarians may be able to subsist on Jarlsberg or other Norwegian cheeses. Vegans are likely to be utterly miserable unless they've stocked up on protein bars and/or peanut butter. Some traditional soups do not contain meat or fish (although they are often prepared with meat stock). Most towns have pizza places, and an occasional Middle Eastern or Chinese restaurant can be found. A good strategy might be to fill up at breakfast, which is usually a buffet featuring cheese, bread, yogurt and fruit (as well as fish and meat).

Norwegian is the national language. Most Norwegians can speak at least minimal English, although they appreciate attempts to speak their language.

Norwegian

I would like something without _____.	Jeg vil gjerne ha noe uten _____.	yay veel YEHR-nuh hah noo-weh EW-tehn _____
We would like something without _____.	Vi vil gjerne ha noe uten _____.	vee veel YEHR-nuh hah noo-weh EW-tuhn _____
I do not eat _____.	Jeg spiser ikke _____.	yay SPEE-suhr EEK-kuh _____
I eat _____ and _____.	Jeg spiser _____ og _____.	yay SPEE-suhr _____ oah _____
meat	kjøtt	hyuht
chicken	kylling	SHEW-ling
fish	fisk	feesk
eggs	egg	ehg
cheese	ost	oost
I am a vegetarian.	Jeg er vegetarianer.	yayg ahr veh-geh-tah-ree-AH-nuhr
Thank you.	Takk.	tahk

Sweden

Traditional Swedish meals are centered around fish (or meat) and potatoes. However, there are many vegetarians and vegans in Sweden. Stockholm proudly offers several specialist vegetarian restaurants and most Swedish cities have at least one. Many restaurants offer at least one or two meatless dishes. In addition, there is a slew of pizzerias, and Chinese, Middle Eastern, and Indian restaurants in the cities. One need not go ethnic, however; it is easy to fill up on buffets at breakfast (bread, cereal, jams, eggs, spreads, yogurt) and *smörgåsbords* at lunch (cheese, eggs, salads, and potatoes, in addition to less-welcome herring and cold cuts). Sweden also offers an array of interesting traditional soups, such as fruit soup, although these can be hard to find in restaurants.

Although Sweden is a decent country for the vegetarian traveler, it can occasionally be difficult to find something meatless to munch, especially in rural areas and in the far north. Herring is omnipresent, so fish-eaters will never lack for something to eat. Salads are served most places, and Swedish dairy products such as yogurt are available everywhere. Sweden produces interesting and unique berries, such as the Arctic cloudberry (which is available out of season in preserves).

Swedish is the national language. English is spoken by a majority of the population as a second language.

Swedish

English	Swedish	Pronunciation
I would like something without _____.	Jag skulle önska någonting utan _____.	yahg skew-luh URN-skuh NOH-goon-teeng EW-tahn _____
We would like something without _____.	Vi skulle önska någonting utan _____.	vee skew-luh URN-skuh NOH-goon-teeng EW-tahn _____

I do not eat ____.	Jag äter inte ____.	yahg EH-tehr IHN-teh ____
I eat ____ and ____.	Jag äter ____ och ____.	yahg EH-tehr ____ awk ____
meat	kött	shuhrt
chicken	höna	HUHR-nuh
fish	fisk	fihsk
eggs	ägg	ehg
cheese	ost	oost
I am a vegetarian.	Jag är vegitarian.	yahg ehr veh-geh-tah-ree-AHN
Thank you	Tack.	tuhk

Switzerland

Swiss food is usually quite heavy and filling with meat as the favorite centerpiece of a meal. But the Swiss also make many potato dishes, such as *rösti* (a potato pancake), that are filling enough to constitute a main course. Both pasta and pizza are common dishes in restaurants, and more creative meatless dishes are becoming more available. A few exclusively vegetarian restaurants have begun to open in Swiss cities. Outside the cities, the abundance of renowned Swiss cheese will keep non-vegan stomachs happy and cholesterol levels skyrocketing. Switzerland, after all, is home to fondue and other cheese dishes such as *raclette* (melted cheese over potatoes or bread) which tastes better than it sounds.

If ponderous Swiss food becomes wearisome, restaurants and fast-food stands in cities and resort areas provide welcome relief with more international offerings, such as Middle Eastern, Greek, or Indian food.

Switzerland has three official languages. In the west of the country, **French** (p. 60) is the principal language. **Italian** (p. 64) is spoken in parts of the south. A very few people speak a Romance language called Romansch, while the majority of Swiss speak various **German** (p. 47) dialects, some of which are nearly impossible for outsiders to understand. (Instead of using coded transmissions, the Swiss army sometimes uses soldiers from remote mountain areas as radio operators.) Most people who have to deal with tourists regularly speak English.

The food of tiny **Liechtenstein** is virtually indistinguishable from that of Switzerland. The language is a dialect of German.

B. Southern Europe

Southern Europe presents something of a paradox to the discerning vegetarian. Generally speaking, traditional Southern European cooking relies less on meat as a central ingredient than other European cuisines do. On the other hand, intentional vegetarianism is still an object of bewilderment to many people in this part of the world. So, while it is usually not difficult to find something meatless to eat, there is a relative scarcity of specialty vegetarian restaurants. In some cases, it may take some searching to find wholly vegetarian entrees, free of meat stock and devoid of random bits of meat or fish. Pesco-vegetarians should have no difficulty anywhere near the Mediterranean Sea, and stricter vegetarians always have the solace of a beautiful climate and abundant fruit and vegetables.

France

French cooking combines aspects of both the Northern European meat fixation and the lighter tradition of Mediterranean cooking.

The result is a cusine that is both highly regarded and highly regional. One problem is that the French thriftily use almost every edible portion of an animal and process it into a variety of sometimes innocuous-seeming items. This makes eating unfamiliar food the gastronomic equivalent of navigating a mine field.

Generally, people in northern France consume more meat but intentional vegetarianism is more commonly practiced here. Most cities and large towns have vegetarian or health restaurants. In addition (happily), many entrees in ordinary French restaurants are free of meat, fish, and mystery organs, and of course bakeries and *patisseries* always offer enticing carbohydrates. In the south of France, fish is a more important part of the diet. This is good news for fish-eaters, irrelevant information for anyone else. Meals become lighter in the south, fresh vegetables and fruits are more prevalent, and the influence of nearby Italy emerges in the form of pasta dishes. There are relatively few vegetarian restaurants here, but the wider use of green growing things in everyday cooking makes this scarcity less of an obstacle.

While it seems almost criminal to come to France and avoid French cooking entirely, in the towns and cities a variety of foreign cuisines are available as an alternative—or temporary change of pace. North African, Middle Eastern, and southeast Asian are the most common due to French colonization patterns, but many other cuisines are represented. And it is perfectly possible (and by no means unpleasant) to subsist on French bread, cheese, fruit, yogurt and of course wine, all of which are available even in the most remote villages whose inhabitants would sooner eat a duck than throw it some crumbs of bread.

French is the official language. Some visitors to Paris may find themselves the subject of ridicule for not speaking French or—almost as sinful—for speaking it improperly. The situation, however, is considerably more relaxed outside the capital and most attempts to speak the language will be welcomed. Basque (p. 72) is spoken in a few areas in the far southeast, some Italian (p. 64) and

Catalan (p. 71) is spoken in the southwest, and German (p.47) is common in Alsace-Lorraine. Arabic (p. 112) is spoken by many immigrants from North Africa.

French

I would like something without _____.	Je voudrais manger quelque chose sans _____.	zhuh voo-dray mahn-zhay kelk shohs sahn _____
We would like something without _____.	Nous voudrions manger quelque chose sans _____.	noo voo-dree-ohn mahn-zhay kelk shohs sahn _____
meat	viande	vee-ohnd
chicken	poulet	poo-lay
fish	poisson	pwahs-sawn
eggs	d'oeufs	zuhrf
cheese	fromage	froh-mahzh
I do not eat _____.	Je ne mange pas _____.	zhuh nuh mahnzh pah _____
meat	de viande	duh vee-ohnd
chicken	de poulet	duh poo-lay
fish	de poisson	duh pwahs-sawn
eggs	d'oeufs	duhrf

cheese	de fromage	duh froh-mahzh
I eat ____ and ____.	Je mange ____ et ____.	zhuh mahnzh ____ ay ____
meat	la viande	lah vee-ohnd
chicken	le poulet	luh poo-lay
fish	le poisson	luh pwahs-sawn
eggs	les oeufs	lay zuhrf
cheese	le fromage	luh froh-mahzh
I am a vegetarian. *(male speaker)*	Je suis végétarien.	zhuh swee vay-zhay-tah-ree-yehn
I am a vegetarian. *(female speaker)*	Je suis végétari-enne.	zhuh swee vay-zhay-tah-ree-yehnn
Please.	Si'l vous plaît.	seel voo play
Thank you.	Merci.	MAYR-see

Monaco's cuisine is very much like that of southern France. High-end international cuisine is common. French is the official language.

Greece

While meaty *souvlaki* and *gyros* are the most familiar represen-

61

tatives of Greek cuisine, there are a variety of meatless dishes available to vegetarian travelers to Greece. These dishes, which typically contain rice, eggplant, or assorted vegetables, may not always be available at restaurants targeted at tourists. Fish-eaters will have no problem along the coast and on the islands (in other words, most of Greece), where fish or shellfish is the usual main course. (Unfortunately for stricter vegetarians, menu variety may consist of having several species of fish from which to choose, rather than offering anything that could be classified as "non-fish.") Even in such fishy circumstances, snacks such as cheese pies and *spanakopita* (spinach turnovers), are ubiquitous, and Greek salad is served at almost every restaurant. An execellent option exists at almost all *tavernas* where a wide variety of appetizers are served, many of which do not contain meat and can be put together to make a substantial meal. Pizza and pasta are also quite common menu items.

Greek is the national language of Greece. It should be noted that the Greek word for vegetarian literally means "vegetable-eater," and is sometimes used as a synonym for crazy so be careful not to use the word out of context!

Greek

The phrases below have been transliterated from the Greek alphabet.

I would like something without ____.	Tha íthela káti horís ____.	thah EE-theh-lah KAH-tee khoh-REESE ____
We would like something without ____.	Tha thélame káti horís ____.	thah THEH-lah-meh KAH-tee khoh-REESE ____

I do not eat ____.	Dhén tróyo ____.	thehnn TROH-oh ____
I eat ____ and ____.	Tróyo ____ ke ____.	TROH-oh ____ keh ____.
meat	kréas	KREH-ahss
chicken	kotópoulo	koh-TOH-poo-loh
fish	psári	PSAH-ree
eggs	avgó	ahv-GHOH
cheese	tirí	tee-REE
I am a vegetarian. *(male speaker)*	Íme hortophágos.	EE-meh hohr-toh-FAH-khohss
I am a vegetarian. *(female speaker)*	Íme hortophága.	EE-meh hohr-toh-FAH-khah
Please.	Parakaló.	pah-rah-kah-LOH
Thank you.	Efkaristó.	ehf-khah-ree-STOH

Italy

Volumes have been written on Italian cuisine so there is certainly no need for this book to launch into an in-depth analysis of the differences between the cuisine of Tuscany and Lombardy. It is sufficient to note that cooking in Italy varies dramatically from region to region, but the one constant—and friend to vegetarians throughout the world—is pasta. While both the form of the pasta and the accompanying ingredients change, it should usually be possible to find some meatless, pasta-based dish almost anywhere in Italy. Salads are devoured everywhere, and Italian breads and cheeses are legendary. Vegans may have trouble, although pasta with tomato sauce and no cheese is common. Some pizzas are made without cheese, especially in southern Italy where often only vegetable toppings are used. There are also many meatless side dishes and *antipasti* and vegetable soups such as minestrone are very common. Be aware though that soups are sometimes made with chicken or meat stock, as are other apparently innocuous dishes such as risotto.

Although there are many meatless Italian dishes, vegetarianism as a deliberate practice is not always understood in Italy. In the cities, especially in the north, there are some specifically vegetarian restaurants. More meat is consumed in the north, where veal, lamb, and chicken dishes are particularly prevalent. In a few cases, a restaurant may offer no meatless dishes at all. In the south, as well as in seaside resorts throughout the country, fish is more prominent. A North African influence becomes evident in Sicily and the far south, where rice, couscous, and lentil soup are common.

Italian is the national language. Although there are many regional dialects, the "standard" Italian given below should be understood everywhere.

Italian

I would like something without ____.	Vorrei qualcosa senza ____.	vohr-RAYee kwahl-KOH-sah SAYN-tsah ____
We would like something without ____.	Vorremmo qualcosa senza ____.	vohr-RAY-moh kwahl-KOH-sah SAYN-tsah ____

I do not eat ____.	Non mangio ____.	nohn MAHN-joh ____
I eat ____ and ____.	Mangio ____ e ____.	MAHN-joh ____ ay ____
meat	carne	KAHR-nay
chicken	pollo	POH-loh
fish	pesce	PAY-shay
eggs	uova	oo-OH-vah
cheese	formaggio	fohr-MAHD-joh
I am a vegetarian. *(female speaker)*	Sono vegetariana.	SOH-noh vay-jay-tah-ree-AH-nah
I am a vegetarian. *(male speaker)*	Sono vegetariano.	SOH-noh vay-jay-tah-ree-AH-noh
Please.	Per favore.	pehr fah-VOH-ray
Thank you.	Grazie.	GRAH-tsee-eh

San Marino and Vatican City are tiny, nominally independent countries wholly surrounded by Italy. Vatican City is only one mile square, so apart from the Vatican snack shops, the only food you are likely to encounter will be spiritual. The food in San Marino is like that of northern Italy. Italian is the language of both countries. Due to the global influence of the Catholic

Church, many other languages are spoken by the few residents of Vatican City.

Malta

Although Malta is a tiny cluster of islands, it has a unique cuisine that blends Arab, Turkish, and Italian influences. Most restaurants, however, cater to tourists, and serve French and Italian food. Traditional Maltese cooking tends to include such non-treats as rabbit and lamb, as well as plenty of fish (these are islands, after all). But surprisingly many options for vegetarians exist. Pasta such as spaghetti and traditional Maltese *ravjul* (ravioli) is available everywhere. There are many vegetable and bean soups, and a host of tangy sheep and goat cheeses. Bread with olive oil is served at every meal and sometimes as a snack, and most local or international-style restaurants serve an array of salads and vegetable appetizers. A common ware of street vendors and bars is *pastizzi*, a pastry filled with cheese or vegetables (but occasionally with meat or fish).

The official languages are **English** and **Maltese**. Although most Maltese are proficient in English, you might find it useful to be able to say a few words of Maltese, especially on the outer islands.

Maltese

I do not eat _____.	Ma niekolx _____.	mah nih-KOHLSH
meat	laħam	LAH-hahm
chicken	ħut	hoot
fish	tiġieġ	TEE-jeech
eggs	bajd	byte

cheese	ġobon	JOH-bohn
I am a vegetarian. *(female speaker)*	Jiena veġetarjana.	yeh-nah veh-jeh-tahr-YAH-nah
I am a vegetarian. *(male speaker)*	Jiena veġetarjan.	yeh-nah veh-jeh-TAHR-yahn
Thank you.	Grazzi.	GRAH-tsee

Portugal

Alas, Portugal is one of the least vegetarian-friendly countries in Southern Europe. The standard Portuguese diet is heavy on chicken, pork, and seafood—especially seafood. While pesco-vegetarians will be delighted, stricter vegetarians may have a difficult time in Portugal. There are a few vegetarian or vegetarian-friendly restaurants in Lisbon, Oporto, and in the resorts of the Algarve on the south coast. The cities also have a selection of restaurants serving other European, Middle Eastern, or Asian cuisines. Apart from these limited options, vegetarians may be restricted to salads, bread, cheese (or cheese sandwiches), fruit, and assorted vegetable side dishes. There are also plenty of vegetable soups on offer, although they often are based on stock or even may contain bits of meat "for flavor."

The national language is **Portuguese**. Although Portuguese as spoken in Brazil is perfectly intelligible to someone from Portugal, there are some differences in pronunciation. Therefore, Portuguese as spoken in Portugal is presented here separately.

Portuguese

I would like something without ____.	Eu gostaria de algo sem ____.	eyoo gohsh-tah-REE-ah duh AHL-goo saym ____

We would like something without _____.	Nos gostariamos de algo sem _____.	noosh goosh-tah-ree-AH-mohs duh AHL-goo saym _____
I do not eat _____.	Eu não como _____.	eyoo now KOH-moo _____
I eat _____ and _____.	Eu como _____ e _____.	eyo KOH-moo _____ ee _____
meat	carne	KAHR-nuh
chicken	frango	FRAYN-goo
fish	peixe	PAY-shuh
eggs	ovos	AW-voos
cheese	queijo	KAY-zhoo
I am a vegetarian. *(female speaker)*	Eu sou vegetariana.	eyoo soh vay-zhay-tah-ree-AH-nah
I am a vegetarian. *(male speaker)*	Eu sou vegetariano.	eyoo soh vay-zhay-tah-ree-AH-noo
Please.	Faz favor.	fahsh fah-VOHR
Thank you. *(male speaker)*	Obrigado.	aw-bree-GAH-doo
Thank you. *(female speaker)*	Obrigada.	aw-bree-GAH-dah

Spain

To a large extent, the exact range of dishes available in Spain depends on the region, but vegetarian entrees are not particularly common anywhere in Spain. In Barcelona, and to a lesser extent in Madrid and other large cities, some specialty vegetarian restaurants exist. In addition, restaurants that are accustomed to northern European tourists, especially more upscale establishments, are likely to offer at least one vegetarian entree. The Middle Eastern and North African restaurants found in most large towns also usually serve meatless dishes.

Otherwise, however, vegetarians face slim pickings. In Andalucia and along the coasts, fish is the most common meal centerpiece, which is good news for pesco-vegetarians. Elsewhere, chicken, pork, or beef are usual. There are often meatless side dishes; rice is reasonably common throughout the country, especially in the south where Arabic influence is greatest. Pizza, salads, or the Spanish *tortilla* (a potato omelette) are all frequently encountered. And in almost every bar, restaurant, or snack shop, the cheese sandwich provides a final option (except for vegans).

The best informal option for vegetarians probably is to indulge in *tapas*, assorted inexpensive appetizers which are available in most bars in the evening. Many *tapas* are meatless, and are often far more interesting than main dishes served in nearby restaurants. If enough of them are eaten, *tapas* make a substantial meal.

The national language of Spain is **Castillian Spanish**. Most people in the country can understand the Castillian dialect, although Andalucian usage is more like that of Latin American Spanish (p. 14). There are also several distinct regional languages. **Catalan** is spoken in Barcelona and the rest of Catalonia, as well as in Valencia and on the Balearic Islands. **Basque,** which is unrelated to any other European language, is spoken in the Basque country of the western Pyrenees and along much of the coast of the Bay of Biscay. Other languages such as Galician are also spoken.

Spanish

I would like something without _____.	Quisiera comer algo sin _____.	kee-see-YAIR-uh koh-MAIR AHL-goh seen _____
We would like something without _____.	Quisieramos comer algo sin _____.	kee-see-YAIR-ah-mohs koh-MAIR AHL-goh seen _____
I do not eat _____.	No como _____.	noh KOH-moh _____
I eat _____ and _____.	Como _____ y _____.	KOH-moh _____ ee _____
meat	carne	KAHR-nay
chicken	pollo	POHL-yoh
fish	pescado	peh-SKAH-doh
eggs	huevos	WAY-bohs
cheese	queso	KAY-soh
I am a vegetarian. *(female speaker)*	Soy vegetariana.	soy beh-heh-tah-ree-AH-nah
I am a vegetarian. *(male speaker)*	Soy vegetariano.	soy beh-heh-tah-ree-AH-noh
Please.	Por favor.	pohr fah-BOHR

70

Thank you.	Gracias.	GRAH-thee-ahs

Catalan

Catalan is divided into various dialects. The phrases below should be generally understood, although local usage may be different.

I do not eat ____.	No menjo ____.	noh MEHN-zhoo ____
I eat ____ and ____.	Menjo ____ i ____.	MEHN-zhoo ____ ee ____
meat	carn	kahrn
chicken	pollastre	puhl-YAH-struh
fish	peix	pehsh
eggs	ous	AW-oos
cheese	formatge	foor-MAHT-zhuh
I am a vegetarian. *(male speaker)*	Soc vegetariá.	sohk buh-zhuh-tuh-ree-AH
I am a vegetarian. *(female speaker)*	Soc vegetariana.	sohk buh-zhuh-tuh-ree-AH-nuh
Please.	Si us plau.	see oos plow
Thank you. *or*	Gracies. Merces.	GRAH-see-uhs muhr-SEHS

71

Basque

Basque usage and pronunciation vary from region to region but the phrases below should be understood by most Basque-speaking people.

I do not eat _____.	Nik ez dut _____ jaten.	nihk ehs doot _____ HAH-tehn
	or	
		nihk ehs doot _____ YAH-tehn
meat	okelarik	oh-KEH-lah-reek
chicken	ollokirik	oh-LOK-kih-reek
fish	arralnik	ahr-RAHL-neek
eggs	arraultzarik	ahr-ROWLTS-ah-reek
cheese	gaztarik	GAHS-tah-reek
I am vegetarian.	Begetarianoa nalz.	beh-geh-tah-ree-AH-noh-ah nahls
Please.	Mezedez.	mehs-EH-dehs
Thank you.	Eskerrik asko.	eh-SKAYR-rihk AH-skoh

The food of small, mountainous **Andorra** is largely oriented towards meat. There are both French and Spanish/Catalonian influences in the cuisine, but Andorra's status as a tourist mecca insures that a variety of cuisines are represented (notably the "international cuisine" of resort areas). Catalan is the official language, but both French (p. 60) and Castillian Spanish are widely spoken.

Gibraltar, a British colony, offers seafood and rather undistinguished fast food, fish and chips, and "John Bull"-themed pubs. English is spoken everywhere in this tiny colony (although most people can speak Spanish too).

C. Central and Eastern Europe

Central and Eastern Europeans generally combine a love for meat with an economic inability to pay for large quantities of it. This combination poses a double threat to vegetarians. First, meat is likely to launch a surprise attack, appearing not as an obvious slab of beef but as a hunk of ham bone in your soup. Second, puzzled, frustrated carnivores may misunderstand you, or worse, treat you as a fool, a dilettante, or a religious freak. Another problem is that, to some extent, the concept "meatless" is different than in the rest of Europe: if a dish is not *mostly* meat, it may be considered *not* meat.

Fortunately, this situation is slowly changing, especially among young people. While there are still few specialty vegetarian restaurants in this part of the world, many ordinary restaurants (especially in urban areas) are beginning to offer meatless entrees, and somewhat less contempt is aimed at people who request them.

Many Eastern European countries actually have a long tradition of meatless cooking during Eastern Orthodox fasts. During Orthodox Easter and at certain other times (in some cases totaling half the year), meat was forbidden for religious reasons, and a whole range of grain, vegetable, and legume dishes developed (the consumption of which sometimes extended to people of other religions). You would be lucky to find these dishes offered in restaurants today, but they do exist. As a final option, you may want to look out for "milk bars," lacto-vegetarian restaurants. Milk bars were common during the Communist era in many Eastern Bloc countries and some are still in operation today.

Albania

Albanian food is not the most interesting cuisine in the world, nor is it particularly vegetarian-friendly. Meat (or fish, along the coast) is the standard restaurant entree. Vegetarians will be more interested in accompaniments, usually vegetables which have frequently, but not always, been boiled to death. Because of the proximity of Italy and Greece, both pasta and Greek salad are common dishes, and pizza is becoming more popular. Although Albania is predominately Muslim, there are many grain and legume dishes that were created for the Eastern Orthodox fasting periods. These dishes can sometimes be found in the countryside.

Albanian is the principal language, but it is spoken in several different dialects. Many Albanians have learned Italian from watching Italian television.

Albanian

In Albania, a nod means no; shaking one's head side to side means yes.

I would like something without _____.	Unë dëshiroj diçka pa ____.	oon duh-shih-roy DEECH-kah pah ____
We would like something without _____.	Ne dëshirojme diçka pa ____.	neh duh-shih-roym DEECH-kah pah ____
I do not eat _____.	Unë nuk ha ____.	oon nook kah ____

I eat ____	Unë ha ____	oon hah ____
and ____.	dhe ____.	thuh ____
meat	mish	meesh
chicken	pulë	pool
fish	peshk	pehshk
eggs	vezë	vehz
cheese	djathë	dyahth
I am a vegetarian.	Unë jam vegjetarian.	oon yahm veh-gyeh-tah-ree-uhn
Please.	Te lutem.	teh loot-ehm
Thank you.	Faleminderit.	fah-leh-meen-deh-reet

Belarus

To most Belarusians, vegetarianism remains an extremely foreign, almost incomprehensible idea; veganism is utterly beyond the pale. There are a very few places in the big cities which serve vegetarian entrees. Away from these rare establishments, you probably will have to make due with vegetable side dishes. The range of options is much like those in Russia: potato concoctions, such as potato pancakes, and other root vegetables (primarily parsnips and beets) are the most common items. Fresh fruit and green vegetables make fairly rare appearances in most restaurants, even in the summer. Bread and dairy products such as curds and *kefir* (a liquid, yogurt-like substance) are fairly good, and can provide the centerpiece of a non-vegan diet if all else fails.

Russian (p. 99) is understood everywhere. The traditional national language is Belarusian, but most people use Russian even in everyday conversation. Indeed, many ethnic Belarusians can only speak Russian.

Bosnia and Herzegovina

As in most of the former Yugoslav republics, the range of options available to vegetarians in Bosnia and Herzegovina is considerably less than fabulous. Balkan cuisine rarely works wonders with meatless ingredients, and the recent civil war did not improve it at all. There are some interesting noodle dishes available, and items like pizza, pasta, and salad are common, but most entrees contain meat. Side dishes will probably have to suffice for most vegetarians here.

There are some regional differences in cuisine; Serbian areas are likely to have the sort of dishes available in Serbia, Croatian areas will have typical Croatian dishes, while the Bosnian Muslims will eat dishes from both areas as well as some (usually meat-based) concoctions of their own. Grain and lentil-based dishes are sometimes available. Before the war, Sarajevo offered the most cosmopolitan selection of cuisine in the region, and if it succeeds fully in rebuilding it is likely to offer it again. When local fresh produce is available, it tends to be of excellent quality.

Serbian (p. 102) and **Croatian** (p. 80) are the main languages in Bosnia and Herzegovina. Once upon a time, not so very long ago, these were considered the same language—Serbo-Croatian. Now that political realities have intruded on the scene, ethnic Croatians speak Croatian, ethnic Serbs say they speak Serbian, and Bosnian Muslims speak one or the other (although in reality, there is little difference). Some linguists have identified a distinct Bosnian dialect, which uses words that are unique and totally distinct from Serbian or Croatian.

Bulgaria

Although some people are vegetarians for health reasons—they are sick, and are under doctor's orders to abstain from meat—and there are some restaurants that cater to these invalids, vegetarianism in general is not at all common in Bulgaria. Most main dishes in ordinary restaurants contain meat in varying amounts. However, it is possible to make due on side dishes and appetizers. Baked eggplant or other vegetables, sometimes stuffed with meat or cheese, is a common accompaniment. Bulgarians make a variety of interesting hot or cold vegetable soups, but these are sometimes made with stock, or even worse, lard. It is very easy to get salads, especially *shopska salada*, a cucumber salad with feta, tomatoes, olive oil, and peppers. There are also some interesting traditional dishes made with grains, lentils, and nuts; these are now quite uncommon outside of the home and you'll be lucky to find them in a restaurant.

It should be a simple matter to get along by preparing your own food if you choose. Yogurt (*kiselo mlyako*) is available everywhere and is justly renowned. In season, Bulgaria produces a wide array of fruits and vegetables. Bulgarian cheese, which is a white feta-like product made from cow or sheep milk, is also widely available. If self-catering becomes tiresome, in the large cities and the Black Sea resorts there are restaurants serving various European or Asian cuisines, and meatless entrees are sometimes available at these establishments. Snack stands and fast-food restaurants might occasionally offer something edible; pizza is an especially popular snack in Bulgaria, as is *banitsa*, a pastry with a cheese filling (although meat is sometimes used).

Bulgarian is the national language. Russian is the most common second language.

Bulgarian

In Bulgaria, a nod means no; shaking one's head side to side means yes.

The following phrases have been transliterated from the Cyrillic alphabet used in Bulgaria.

I would like something without _____. *(female speaker)*	Az bih iskala nešto bez _____.	ahz bee IHSS-kah-lah NEH-shtoh behz _____
I would like something without _____. *(male speaker)*	Az bih iskal nešto bez _____.	ahz bee IHSS-kahl NEH-shtoh behz _____
We would like something without _____.	Nie bihme iskali nešto bez _____.	nee BEE-meh IHSS-kah-lee NEH-shtoh behz _____
I do not eat _____.	Az ne yam _____.	ahz neh yahm _____
I eat _____ and _____.	Az yam _____ i _____.	ahz yahm _____ ee _____
meat	meso	meh-SOH
chicken	pile	pee-LAY
fish	riba	REE-bah
eggs	yaitse	yai-TZEH
cheese	sirene	SEE-reh-neh
I am a vegetarian. *(male speaker)*	Az sâm vegetarianets.	ahz suhm veh-geh-tah-ree-AH-nehtz

I am a vegetarian. *(female speaker)*	Az sâm vegetarianka.	ahz suhm veh-geh-tah-ree-AHN-kah
Please.	Mola.	MOH-lah
Thank you.	Blagodarya	blah-goh-dahr-YAH

Croatia

The options available to vegetarian visitors in Croatia are quite limited. There are a few vegetarian restaurants in Zagreb, but most restaurants are simply not geared to providing meatless entrees. Italian food is fairly common, particularly along the coast, so pizza and pasta are options in many areas. (Italian food in Croatia sometimes undergoes odd transformations, as with pizza topped with sour cream.) There are also occasional surprises such as Chinese restaurants, which tend to serve at least one or two vegetarian entrees. A few traditional Croatian main dishes are made without meat, but these dishes are usually found only as part of home-cooked meals.

A more reliable strategy for vegetarians is to focus on side dishes, snacks, or *meze* (appetizers). One common example of meze is *ajvar*—a roasted pepper and eggplant spread. Along the Dalmatian coast, *blitva* (chard) sauteed in garlic with new potatoes is a common side dish. Typical snacks are *burek*, a pastry that is usually filled with cheese (but sometimes with meat) or pancakes (including interesting varieties such as spinach pancakes). There are also good bakeries, and fresh produce in the summer and fall is of high quality. Fish is usually the main dish along the coast, so pesco-vegetarians would do well to flock towards the Adriatic.

Croatian, formerly thought of as Serbo-Croatian, is the national language.

Croatian

I would like something without ____. *(female speaker)*	Željela bih nešto bez ____.	ZHEHL-yeh-luh bee NEHSH-toh behz ____
I would like something without ____. *(male speaker)*	Želio bih nešto bez ____.	ZHEH-lee-oh bee NEHSH-toh behz ____
We would like something without ____.	Željeli bih nešto bez ____.	ZHEHL-yeh-lee bee NEHSH-toh behz ____
meat	mesa	MEH-sah
chicken	piletine	PEE-leh-tih-neh
fish	ribe	RREE-beh
eggs	jaja	yah-yah
cheese	sira	SEE-rah
I do not eat ____.	Ne jedem ____.	neh YEH-dehm ____
I eat ____ and ____.	Jedem ____ i ____.	YEH-dehm____ ee ____
meat	meso	MEH-soh
chicken	piletinu	PEE-leh-tih-noo
fish	ribu	RREE-boo

eggs	jaje	yah-yeh
cheese	sir	seer
I am a vegetarian. *(female speaker)*	Ja sam vegetarijanka.	yah sahm veh-geh-tah-ree-YAHN-kuh
I am a vegetarian. *(male speaker)*	Ja sam vegetarijanac.	yah sahm veh-geh-tah-ree-YAH-nahtz
Please.	Molim.	MOH-leem
Thank you.	Hvala.	HVAH-lah

Czech Republic

Although vegetarianism remains uncommon here, it is becoming easier to manage; indeed, the Czech Republic is probably the easiest (or more accurately, the least difficult) of the former Soviet satellites in which to practice vegetarianism. Of course, the normal Czech diet involves meat and plenty of it. Traditionally, Czechs consumed lots of potatoes, and flour or potato dumplings were and are an ubiquitous dish. But the range of options (for Czechs as well as for visitors) has diversified significantly since the Velvet Revolution. Prague has suffered the onslaught of American fast-food, but as a counterpoint several specialty vegetarian restaurants have opened, and there are a burgeoning number of new, vegetarian-friendly restaurants. Restaurants run by or catering to foreigners tend to be especially receptive to vegetarians. (Veganism remains very difficult, however.) Many ordinary restaurants in Prague and Brno now feature a meatless section on the menu.

Speaking Vegetarian

Outside the cities, obtaining vegetarian meals becomes more difficult. In medium-sized and small cities some restaurants have begun to offer vegetarian entrees but in small towns and villages there are few choices. It is often possible to ask for a special meatless meal, and proprietors are likely to be somewhat more receptive to such requests than they would have been just a few years ago. (Be warned that the quality of the resulting entree may not be stellar.) Otherwise, potato and vegetable side dishes will have to suffice. For those who are unconcerned about fat or cholesterol content, fried breaded cheese (*smazeny sýr*) is on virtually every menu. Pesco-vegetarians should be able to get by with ease in most parts of the Czech Republic.

Czech is the national language. German is widely spoken, especially in the western part of the country. English is becoming a popular second language.

Czech

I would like something without _____. *(male speaker)*	Rád bych něco bez ____.	rahd beekh NYEH-tzoh behz ____
I would like something without _____. *(female speaker)*	Ráda bych něco bez ____.	RAH-dah beekh NYEH-tzoh behz ____
We would like something without _____.	Rádi bychom něco bez ____.	RAHD-yee BEE-khohm NYEH-tzoh behz ____
meat	masa	MUH-suh
chicken	kuřete	KOOR-zheh-teh

82

fish	ryby	RIH-bih
eggs	vajec	VAH-yehtz
cheese	sýra	SEE-ruh
I do not eat ___.	Nejím ___.	NEH-yeem ___
I eat ___ **and** ___.	Jím ___ a ___.	yeem ___ uh ___
meat	maso	MUH-soh
chicken	kuřata	KOOR-zhuh-tuh
fish	ryby	RIH-bih
eggs	vejce	VAY-tzeh
cheese	sýr	seer
I am a vegetarian. *(male speaker)*	Jsem vegetarián.	sehm VEH-geh-tuh-ree-ann
I am a vegetarian. *(female speaker)*	Jsem vegetariánka.	sehm VEH-geh-tuh-ree-ann-kuh
Please.	Prosím.	PROH-seem
Thank you.	Děkuji.	DYEH-kuh-yee
We thank you.	Děkujeme.	DYEH-kuh-yeh-meh

Estonia

Of the three Baltic states, Estonia is probably the most accommodating (or the least hostile) to vegetarians. There are several vegetarian or veggie-friendly restaurants in Tallinn, and a few restaurants in other cities are beginning to add the occasional meatless entree to their menus. Pizza is a common snack. Estonians make interesting grain dishes, such as porridges, as well as a variety of fruit or vegetable soups. (Be careful, some soups are made with stock, others are milk-based.) These dishes are only infrequently available in restaurants, however. Similarly, berries, mushrooms, and other forest produce are often collected for use at home, but are rarely encountered in restaurants. Salads and pasta are often available.

Estonian is the official language. Almost a third of the population speaks Russian (p. 99) as a mother tongue, and Latvian and Lithuanian are also occasionally useful.

Estonian

I would like something without ____.	Ma sooviksin midagi ilma____.	mah soo-VIHK-sihn mih-DAH-gih IHL-mah ____
meat	lihata	LEE-hah-tah
chicken	kanata	KAH-nah-tah
fish	kalata	KAH-lah-tah
eggs	munata	MOO-nah-tah
cheese	juusttuta	YOOST-too-tah
I do not eat ____.	Ma ei sőő ____.	mah eye soor ____

84

I eat ____ and ____.	Ma sőőn ____ ja ____.	mah soorn ____ yaa ____
meat	liha	LEE-hah
chicken	kana	KAH-nah
fish	kala	KAH-lah
eggs	muna	MOO-nah
cheese	juustu	YOOST-too
I am a vegetarian.	Ma olen taimetoitlane.	mah oh-LAAN tye-meh-TOH-iht-lah-neh
Please.	Palun.	PAH-loon
Thank you.	Tänan.	TAAN-aan

Hungary

Hungarian food is widely regarded as among the richest and most inventive in all Europe. Although Hungarians have largely restricted their culinary inventiveness to meat-based dishes such as *goulash*, vegetarians will not necessarily go hungry in Hungary. In Budapest, it has become relatively easy to avoid meat. Some vegetarian restaurants have opened in the last few years, and many restaurants are now beginning to offer meatless entrees. Budapest also has an impressive concentration of pizzerias, which can usually provide vegetarian sustenance. Away from Budapest, the pickings become slimmer. Some Hungarian vegetable side dishes are excellent (but beware of overzealous cooks smothering them in lard). Hungarian soups tend to be excellent, although even non-meat soups are usually made with meat stock. Traditional chilled fruit soups are generally (but not always) milk-based. Pesco-vegetarians will find that fish is quite common, and is especially good along Lake Balaton.

Hungarian is the national language.

Hungarian

I would like something without ____.	Szeretnék kérni valamit ____ nélkül.	seh-reht-NAYK KAYR-nee vah-lah-MEET ____ NAYL-kewl
We would like something without ____.	Szeretnénk kérni valamit ____ nélkül.	seh-reht-NAYNK KAYR-nee vah-lah-MEET ____ NAYL-kewl
meat	hús	hoosh
chicken	csirke	CHEER-keh
fish	hal	hahl
eggs	tojás	TOY-ahsh
cheese	sajt	shoyt
I do not eat ____.	Nem eszem ____.	naym EH-sehm ____
I eat ____ and ____.	Eszem ____ és ____.	EH-sehm ____ aysh ____

meat	húst	hoosht
chicken	csirkét	CHEER-kayt
fish	halat	hah-laht
eggs	tojást	TOH-yahsht
cheese	sajtot	shoy-toht
I am a vegetarian.	Vegetáriánus vagyok.	vay-guh-tah-ree-ah-noosh vahd-YOHK
Please.	Kérek.	KAY-rehk
Thank you.	Köszönöm.	kuhr-suhr-nuhm

Latvia

The average Latvian diet is heavy on meat and potatoes. There are a few restaurants in Riga which serve vegetarian entrees, but these are definitely exceptions. Pesco-vegetarians will get by easily, as fresh or smoked fish and eel are easy to find. Stricter vegetarians may struggle. At home, most Latvians cook with whole grains such as buckwheat, oats, or barley, but dishes made with such wholesome ingredients are hard to find in restaurants. As elsewhere in the Baltic states, potatoes in one form or another are popular both at home and in restaurants. Other sturdy vegetables, particularly root crops, are standard Latvian fare. Some grain or vegetable soups, such as barley soup or *biesu* (borscht), may entice, but are often cooked in stock.

If you rely on your own initiative and cooking skills, life will be relatively easy. Wonderful fruit and vegetables are available in summer, and apples are abundant in the fall. (Preserved produce is sometimes available during the rest of the year.) Latvia produces good breads and other baked goods, and dairy products such as cheese, cottage cheese, and yogurt are high quality and easily available. As Latvia progresses economically and gets more exposure to the outside world, vegetarianism will no doubt become easier and more accepted (although probably not commonplace).

Latvian is the official language. A substantial minority of the population speaks Russian (p. 99) as a first language, and most people can speak it as a second language.

Latvian

I would like something without ____.	Es gribētu pasūtīt kautko bez ____.	ehss GREE-bah-too PAH-soo-teet KOWT-koh behz ____
We would like something without ____.	Mēs vēlamies pasūtīt kautko bez ____.	mayss VAH-luh-mees PAH-soo-teet KOWT-koh behz____
meat	gaļas	GAHL-luhss
chicken	vistas	VISS-tahss
fish	zivs	zihvs
eggs	olām	OH-lahm
cheese	siera	SEE-eh-ruh
I do not eat ____.	Es neēdu ____.	ehss NAY-ah-doo ____

I eat _____	Es ēdu _____	ehss AH-doo _____
and _____.	un _____.	uhn _____
meat	gaļu	GAHL-loo
chicken	vistu	VISS-too
fish	zivi	ZEE-vee
eggs	olas	OO-wuh-luhss
cheese	sieru	SEE-eh-roo
Please.	Lūdzu.	LOOD-zoo
Thank you.	Paldies.	pahl-DEE-uhs

Lithuania

Despite some incremental improvements in recent years (and the recent opening of a few vegetarian restaurants), it remains quite difficult to find meatless meals in Lithuania. Part of the problem is misunderstanding: for example, many so-called "vegetarian" pizzas are made with ham. Another part of the problem is resentment bred from years of deprivation, which causes otherwise friendly and rational people to view vegetarianism as new age, self-indulgent, insulting behavior. This general hostility is especially unfortunate because Lithuanians make some very good food without meat. Mushrooms, berries, and other forest produce are traditional ingredients in many homemade Lithuanian dishes, but these are rarely available in restaurants. Porridges and vegetable soups provide another meatless option, but again these are hard to find outside of homes.

Boiled potatoes, while not particularly exciting, are at least

Speaking Vegetarian

meat-free and accompany most main dishes. There are a host of more elaborate potato dishes such as pancakes and dumplings, but many of these are mixed with some form of meat. Pasta and really excellent breads are easily available, and salads are becoming more common than they once were. If you cook for yourself, local fruit and vegetables are wonderful in season. Pesco-vegetarians should have no problems here: fish, especially herring, is ubiquitous.

Lithuanian is the official language. Russian (p. 99) is widely spoken as a second language, and the Russian ethnic minority within the country speaks it as a first language. There is also a Polish-speaking minority.

Lithuanian

I would like something without ____.	Aš norėčiau ką nors be___.	uhsh noh-REH-chow kah nohrrs beh ____
We would like something without ____.	Mes norėtumėm ką nors be___.	mahs noh-REH-tuh-mehm kah nohrrs beh ____
meat	mėsos	MAY-sohs
chicken	vištienos	vihsh-TYEH-nohs
fish	žuvies	zhoo-VEES
eggs	kiaušinių	kee-ow-SHINN-yoo
cheese	sūrio	SOO-rih-oh
I do not eat ____.	Aš nevalgau ___.	uhsh neh-VUHL-gow ____

90

I eat _____ and _____.	Aš valgau___ir___.	uhsh VUHL-gow _____ ihr_____
meat	mėsą	MAY-sah
chicken	vištieną	vihsh-TYEH-nah
fish	zŭvį	ZHOO-vee
eggs	kiaušinius	kee-ow-SHINN-yuhs
cheese	sūrį	SOO-ree
I am a vegetarian. *(male speaker)*	Aš esu vegetaras.	uhsh eh-SOO veh-geh-TAH-ruhs
I am a vegetarian. *(female speaker)*	Aš esu vegetarė.	uhsh eh-SOO veh-geh-TAH-ray
Please.	Prašau.	prahsh-OW
Thank you.	Ačiu.	AH-choo

Macedonia

Although some meatless food is available, Macedonia remains a difficult place to find vegetarian meals. For economic reasons, most Macedonians tend to avoid using much meat at home but this vegetarianism is generally forced, not intentional; very few people here are vegetarians by choice. Most restaurants specialize in meat, reasoning that their patrons usually eat vegetarian food at home and are looking for a change. Fortunately, interesting vegetable side dishes are often available, some the result of Turkish or Greek influence: Greek salads, eggplant, and cheese or spinach pastries are all fairly typical. The few restaurants that are used to foreigners are more likely to offer meatless entrees. Pizza is a common snack food, and pasta is sometimes available at restaurants. Self-caterers are likely to be favorably impressed with the quality of Macedonian produce in season.

Macedonian is the main national language. Macedonia uses both the Cyrillic and the Roman alphabet, although Cyrillic is more commonly used. A large minority of the population speaks Albanian (p. 74), particularly in the west. Serbian is also widely spoken, and is the most common second language.

Macedonian

The phrases below are presented in the Roman alphabet only.

I would like something without _____. *(male speaker)*	Bi sakal nesto bez_____.	bee SAH-kahl NEHSH-toh behz ____
I would like something without _____. *(female speaker)*	Bi sakala nesto bez ____.	bee SAH-kah-lah NEHSH-toh behz ____
We would like something without _____.	Bi sakale nesto bez ____.	bee SAH-kah-leh NEHSH-toh behz ____
I do not eat _____.	Ne jadam ____.	neh YAH-dahm ____
I eat _____ and _____.	Jadam ____ i ____.	YAH-dahm ____ ee ____

meat	meso	MEH-soh
chicken	kokoska	KOH-kohsh-kah
fish	riba	REE-bah
eggs	jajca	yai-tsah
cheese	sirenje	SEE-rehn-yeh
I am a vegetarian. *(male speaker)*	Jas sum vegetarijanec.	yahss soom veh-geh-tah-ree-YAH-nehts
I am a vegetarian. *(female speaker)*	Jas sum vegetarijanka.	yahss soom veh-geh-tah-ree-YAHN-kah
Please.	Molam.	MOH-lahm
Thank you.	Blagodaram.	blah-GOH-dah-rahm

Moldova

Despite (or because of) their relative poverty, few Moldovans are voluntary vegetarians, and many common dishes contain pieces of meat in some form. Nonetheless, it is possible to subsist on Moldova's national dish, *mamalagia*, an orange-colored cornmeal mush similar to polenta. It is usually served with meat or vegetable stew or feta cheese. Sometimes fried vegetables are available, and pasta and pizza are occasionally found. Upscale restaurants are more likely (though not guaranteed) to have vegetarian options. A variety of vegetable soups appear on menus, but these are often made with stock. Bread is quite good and very hearty, and Moldovan produce is excellent when it is available.

Moldovan is the official language. It is virtually identical to

Romanian (p. 97) in all important respects. Russian is also widely spoken. A small minority of the population speaks a Turkish dialect.

Poland

Poland has a long list of traditional dishes that are prepared without meat, and contain pulses such as lentils, mushrooms and other forest produce, or grains such as buckwheat. These dishes can be hard to find at restaurants, however, since, as Poland grows wealthier, traditional food is maligned as "peasant food" and meat consumption is skyrocketing after years of rationing and privation. Indeed, many Poles (predominantly older people) find vegetarianism as a conscious choice to be an utterly incomprehensible concept. At the same time, however, vegetarianism is becoming more common, especially among young people. Warsaw, Krakow, and other large cities now have vegetarian restaurants and many restaurants in urban areas, particularly more upscale establishments, are adding vegetarian entrees to their menus.

The cities also offer some ethnic choices, such as Chinese restaurants. Salad bars are becoming popular (but watch out for meat in salads).

Outside the cities, it is much more difficult to find meatless food. Some towns still have milk bars (dairy restaurants) left over from the Communist era, but these are dying off. Pizza is a common snack food, but Polish pizza tends to be appallingly bad. Soups are sometimes a good option, although they are often made with stock or may even contain bits of meat. Polish borscht is usually vegetarian, unlike the versions served in countries further east. Starchy side dishes may come to the rescue; potatoes and potato pancakes are very common, and some *pierogi* (dumplings) are meatless. Yogurt and other dairy products are widely available.

Polish is the national language. Russian is the most common second language.

Some English is spoken in the cities, but it is not widely spoken in rural areas.

Polish

I would like something without _____.	Proszę coś bez _____.	PROH-sheh tsohsh behz _____
We would like something without _____.	Prosimy coś bez_____.	proh-SHEE-mih oh tsohsh behz _____
I do not eat _____.	Nie jem _____.	nyeh yehm _____
meat	mięsa	mee-EHN-sah
chicken	kury	KOO-rih
fish	ryby	rrih-bih
eggs	jajek	yai-YEK
cheese	sera	sehr-ah
I eat _____ and _____.	Jem _____ i _____.	yehm _____ ee _____
meat	mięso	mee-EHN-soh
chicken	kurę	KOO-rreh
fish	ryby	rrih-bih
eggs	jajka	yai-KAH
cheese	ser	sehr

I am a vegetarian. *(male speaker)*	Jestem wegetarianinem.	YEH-stehm veh-geh-tah-rree-ah-NIHN-ehm
I am a vegetarian. *(female speaker)*	Jestem wegetarianiną.	YEH-stehm veh-geh-tah-rree-ah-NIHN-ahn
Please.	Proszę.	PROH-sheh
Thank you.	Dziękuję.	jyehn-KOO-yehn

Romania

Meat is too expensive for the average Romanian to eat on a daily basis, so the majority of Romanians are unwilling vegetarians. Those who can afford to eat out generally go "whole hog" for meat, so to speak. Nonetheless, most restaurants that cater to tourists (generally more pricey establishments) will offer vegetarian entrees. Romania formerly had many lacto-vegetarian restaurants serving, as the name implies, meatless food that often included dairy products. These restaurants were originally meant for people who were on a meatless diet by doctor's orders. Most are now private enterprises and serve meat, although some meatless dishes can still be had.

At ordinary restaurants the choices for vegetarians are limited. There are plenty of vegetable soups and stews, but these usually use meat stock or contain bits of meat. Pasta is reasonably common. The most distinctive Romanian dish is probably *mamaliga*, cornmeal mush served with cheese or milk. It should be noted that religious Romanians avoid meat, and sometimes all animal products, two days per week throughout the year, and for weeks at a time during Lent, the pre-Christmas period, and parts of June and August. Monasteries serve meatless (sometimes entirely vegan) dishes at these times and some restaurants expand their menus to include more meatless dishes during these periods.

The official language is **Romanian**; a Romance language, it sits forlornly among the mostly Slavic languages of Eastern Europe. The Hungarian ethnic minority speaks Hungarian (p. 86).

Romanian

I would like something without ____.	Asi dori ceva fără ____.	ahsh doh-REE jeh-VAAH FUH-ruh ____
We would like something without ____.	Am dori ceva fără ____.	ahm doh-REE jeh-VAAH FUH-ruh ____
I do not eat ____.	Nu mănâc ____.	noo MUH-newnk ____
I eat ____ and ____.	Mănânc ____ și ____.	MUH-newnk ____ shee ____
meat	carne	KAHR-nay
chicken	pui	pwee
fish	pește	PAYSH-tay
eggs	ouă	OH-wuh
cheese	brânză	BREWN-zuh
I am a vegetarian. *(male speaker)*	Sunt vegetarian.	soont veh-jeh-tah-ree-yahn
I am a vegetarian. *(female speaker)*	Sunt vegetariană.	soont veh-jeh-tah-ree-yah-nuh

Please.	Vă rog.	vuh rohg
Thank you.	Mulţumesc.	mool-tsoo-MEHSK

Russia

Russians tell an old joke that goes like this: "All Russians are vegetarians! We have no meat, no milk, no eggs . . ." While privation and shortages have long taken their toll on Russian meat consumption, very few Russians are intentional vegetarians, and most think the concept is exceedingly strange. Most restaurants have no meatless entrees at all, and since dairy products are almost always used in the few cases where meat is not, vegans are in a hopeless position. However, attitudes are slowly changing. Many Russians now understand the concept, even if they do not appreciate it; young people in urban areas are most likely to be receptive to the idea.

In Moscow and St. Petersburg, a few vegetarian restaurants have opened up, and some ordinary restaurants have begun to experiment with meatless entrees. Many of the new Western chains that have opened in Russia in the last few years serve vegetarian dishes. There are also a few ethnic restaurants in the large cities serving Chinese, Vietnamese, Middle Eastern, or other cuisines; Georgian or Armenian restaurants are highly regarded, and almost always offer some wonderful meatless entrees. Western European cuisines are also well-represented, but these restaurants tend to be expensive.

Outside the major cities, vegetarian prospects become bleak. There is surprisingly little variation in the type of food available, except in the Caucasus where local cooking becomes more interesting. Potatoes are served as part of almost every meal, and it is certainly possible to subsist on them. Vegetables are usually canned. There are some good soups, but they are typically made with meat stock (even *borscht* is generally meat-based). However, some fruit soups do not contain stock. Cucumber salad, combined with *zakuski* (appetizers), could make a meal. Omelettes are often available, and buckwheat porridge or pancakes can sometimes be found. Dairy products are more easily available than they once were; kefir, yogurt, curds, and cheese are all relatively common and nutritious. Russian bread is also filling and generally good.

Away from the few urban centers, Siberia poses a special challenge. Almost everything contains meat, and fresh vegetables are rare; even canned vegetables are not always available. It is probably best to cook for oneself here. The situation is considerably ameliorated if one can eat fish, which is common in most of Siberia, as well as in the remainder of Russia.

Russian is the official language. There are hordes of minority groups in Russia, especially in the Caucasus, Siberia, and Tatarstan, which speak their own language as a mother tongue, but almost everyone can speak Russian as a second language. Languages listed elsewhere in this book that may come in handy in Russia include Armenian (p. 117), Georgian (p. 122), Azeri (p. 119), Uzbek (p. 210), Kazakh (p. 205), Ukrainian (p.108), or Mongolian (p. 220).

Russian

The following phrases have been transliterated from the Cyrillic alphabet.

I/We would like something without _____.	možno šhto nibud'bez _____.	MAWZH-naw SHTAW nee-bood byehz _____
meat	mjasa	MYAH-suh
chicken	kuritsi	koo-reets-ee
fish	ribi	RRIH-bih
eggs	jaits	yah-eets

cheese	sira	seer-uh
I do not eat ____.	Ja nje kušayu ___.	yah nyeh KOO-shah-yoo____
I eat ____ and ____.	Ja kušayu ___ i ___.	yah KOO-shah-yoo ____ ee ____
meat	mjaso	MYAH-saw
chicken	kuritsu	koo-reets-oo
fish	riboo	RRIH-boo
eggs	jaitsa	yah-eets-uh
cheese	sir	seer
I am a vegetarian. *(male speaker)*	Ja vjegjetjerianjetz.	yah vyeh-gyeh-tyeh-ree-AH-nyehtz
I am a vegetarian. *(female speaker)*	Ja vjegjetjerianka.	yah vyeh-gyeh-tyeh-ree-AHN-kuh
Please.	Požaloojsta.	paw-ZHAHL-stahh
Thank you.	Spasibo.	spah-SEE-baw

Serbia and Montenegro

A common term for Serbia and Montenegro, "rump Yugoslavia," largely sums up the dietary options in this part of the world. Of all former Yugoslav republics, Serbia and Montenegro are probably the least tuned into the outside world. People are unlikely to understand the concept of vegetarianism, which is generally considered bizarre and unhealthy. There are a few restaurants that are beginning to add meatless dishes to their menus, but these are the exceptions. The few meatless options commonly found usually take the form of side dishes, including salads, grilled mushrooms, and the occasional fried or roasted vegetable dish. Most towns have pizzerias, and many restaurants offer pizza or pasta (you will have to tell them to leave off the meat). There are also some traditional noodle and pastry dishes that do not contain meat, and are often delicious. These dishes are often available at snack stands or hole-in-the-wall establishments. Dairy products and bread tend to be adequate and readily available. In season, there is excellent local produce, but usually you will have to prepare this yourself—most restaurants inexplicably fail to take advantage of this bounty.

The boundaries of Serbia and Montenegro remain subject to change; in particular, the status of the mostly ethnically Albanian province of Kosovo is an open question. The cuisine of Kosovo province is more akin to that of Albania (p. 74) than that of Serbia or Montenegro proper.

Serbian is the national language. Although there are some minor differences, it is essentially the same as Croatian (p. 80). Most parts of Serbia use the Cyrillic alphabet; in Montenegro, Roman script is sometimes used (Note: Since we've Romanized the Serbian words, the allusion to Croatian is not necessary). Albanian (p. 74) is spoken in the Kosovo province in the south.

Serbian

The following phrases have been transliterated from the Cyrillic alphabet that most Serbians use.

Serbian

I would like something without _____. (*male speaker*)	Želeo bih nešto bez ____.	ZHEH-leh-oh bee NEHSH-toh behz ____
I would like something without _____. (*female speaker*)	Želela bih nešto bez ____.	ZHEH-leh-lah bee NEHSH-toh behz ____
We would like something without _____.	Želeli bih nešto bez ____.	ZHEH-leh-lee bee NEHSH-toh behz ____
meat	mesa	MEH-sah
chicken	piletine	PEE-leh-tee-neh
fish	ribe	REE-beh
eggs	jaja	yah-yah
cheese	sira	SEE-rah
I do not eat _____.	Ne jedem ____.	neh YEH-dehm ____
I eat _____ and _____.	Jedem ____ i ____.	YEH-dehm ____ ee ____
meat	meso	MEH-saw
chicken	piletinu	PEE-leh-tee-noo

102

fish	ribu	RREE-boo
eggs	jaja	yah-yah
cheese	sir	seer
I am a vegetarian. *(male speaker)*	Ja sam vegetarijanats.	yah sahm veh-geh-tah-REE-yah-nahtz
I am a vegetarian. *(female speaker)*	Ja sam vegetarijanka.	yah sahm veh-geh-tah-REE-yahn-kuh
Please.	Molim.	MOH-leem
Thank you.	Hvala.	HVAH-lah

Slovakia

In Slovakia, meat is the core of a restaurant lunch or dinner, and vegetarianism is rare (although the average Slovak eats little meat at home due to the expense). The hapless diner may be greeted by slabs of beef or pork, or sometimes fish. Despite the general dearth of meatless entrees, there are a couple of vegetarian restaurants in Bratislava, and a few other restaurants are beginning to offer vegetarian entrees (primarily restaurants that cater to foreigners in touristed areas). Away from these veggie-friendly oases, a visiting vegetarian may have to subsist on potatoes or other vegetable side dishes, perhaps (if you are lucky) accompanied by beans or lentils. If you can find it, the Slovak national dish is a sort of dumpling and cheese concoction called *bryndzové halušky*. There also exist a range of potato-based dishes, such as dumplings and potato pancakes, which are commonly served as

103

snacks as well as main dishes. If you resort to cooking for yourself, during the summer and fall you will find wonderful fresh produce at local markets. Slovak bread tends to be quite good.

Slovak is the national language. Although Slovak was often lumped in with Czech before Czechoslovakia split, they are distinct albeit similar languages. Russian is widely spoken as a second language.

Slovak

I would like something without ____. *(female speaker)*	Chcela by som niečo bez ____.	KEH-seh-lah bih sohm NYEH-choh behz ____
I would like something without ____. *(male speaker)*	Chcel by som niečo bez ____.	، KEH-sehl bih sohm NYEH-choh behz ____
We would like something without ____.	Chceli by sme niečo bez ____.	KEH-seh-lih bih smeh NYEH-choh behz ____
meat	mäsa	MEH-suh
chicken	kurčata	KOOR-chuh-tyuh
fish	rýb	reeb
eggs	vajec	VUH-yehts
cheese	syru	SIH-roo

I do not eat _____.	Nejem _____.	NUH-yehm _____
I eat _____ and _____.	Jem _____ a _____.	yehm _____ uh _____
meat	mäso	MEH-soh
chicken	kura	KOO-rah
fish	ryby	REE-bee
eggs	vajcia	VYTES-yuh
cheese	syr	seer
I am a vegetarian. *(female speaker)*	Som vegetariánka.	sohm VEH-geh-tuh-rih-ahn-kah
I am a vegetarian. *(male speaker)*	Som vegetarián.	sohm VEH-geh-tuh-rih-ahn
Please.	Prosím.	PROH-seem
Thank you.	Ďakujem.	DYUH-kuh-yehm
We thank you.	Ďakujeme.	DYUH-kuh-yeh-meh

Slovenia

While vegetarianism is not yet common or widely accepted in Slovenia, it is becoming almost fashionable among young people. Older people are still very resistant to the idea, however, especially in rural areas where pork fat is often used to cook vegetables and grains, and most people eat as much meat as they can get. Still, Slovenia is probably the easiest of the former Yugoslav states for vegetarians. A few vegetarian restaurants are starting to crop up, mainly in Ljubljana. There are many pizza restaurants, most of which offer vegetarian pizzas. Some delis and supermarkets sell vegetarian sandwiches. In conventional restaurants, it is usually a simple matter to construct a meal from vegetable side dishes, and many restaurants have pasta dishes. A common Slovenian snack, *burek* (a flaky turnover) is sometimes made with cheese instead of meat. On the coast, fish-eaters will find plenty of seafood dishes.

Slovene is the national language. Croatian and German are common second languages. Some Italian is spoken along the coast.

Slovene

I would like something without ____.	Želim jesdi nekaj brez ____.	zheh-LEEM YEHSS-dee nay-kye brehz ____
We would like something without ____.	Želimo jesdi nakaj brez ____.	zheh-LEEM-oh YEHSS-dee nay-kye brehz ____
I do not eat ____.	Ne jem ____.	neh yehm ____
meat	mesa	meh-SAH
chicken	piščanca	pees-CHAHN-tsah
fish	ribe	RRIH-beh
eggs	jajc	yites
cheese	sira	see-rah

106

I eat____ and ____.	Jem ____ in ____.	yehm____ een____
meat	meso	meh-SOH
chicken	piščanca	pees-CHAHN-tsah
fish	ribo	RRIH-boh
eggs	jajca	YITE-sah
cheese	sir	seer
I am a vegetarian. *(male speaker)*	Sem vegeterianec.	suhm veh-geh-teh-ree-YAH-nehtz
I am a vegetarian. *(female speaker)*	Sem vegetarianka.	suhm veh-geh-tah-ree-YAHN-kah
Please.	Prosim.	PROH-seem
Thank you.	Hvala.	HVAH-lah

Ukraine

Ukrainians are largely unsympathetic to vegetarians, although this attitude is changing very gradually. Most Ukrainian main dishes contain meat or fish, albeit often in small quantities. Main dishes are usually served with some permutation of potato, whether boiled, made into pancakes, or fashioned into dumplings. Besides the sturdy potato, which may be a vegetarian's best friend in Ukraine, one can find various other grain-based dishes, such as *nalesnyky* (blintzes), buckwheat pancakes, and cheese or vegetable dumplings (although the latter are often filled with or smothered by meat). Perhaps the most common grain dish is *kasha*, a sort of substantial grain porridge, usually made from buckwheat. Hearty bread is served at every meal. Fresh fruit and vegetables can be hard to find, especially out of season; vegetables are easiest to find in the Crimean region.

Some smaller restaurants in Ukraine may offer a traditional meatless specialty (although not from an intentional desire to be vegetarian-friendly). Ukrainian vegetable soups such as *borscht* can be very good, but unfortunately they are usually made with meat broth. For non-vegans, fermented dairy products such as yogurt, *kefir*, or curds are easily available and provide a good way to add variety to the diet.

Ukrainian is the main language. Russian (p. 99) is very widely spoken, and is the first language of the many ethnic Russians who live in southern and eastern Ukraine.

Ukrainian

The following phrases have been transliterated from the Cyrillic alphabet used to write Ukrainian.

I would like something without _____.	Ja khochi schos´ bez _____.	yah **kh**oh-chih sh-chohss behz _____
I do not eat _____.	Ja ne jim _____.	yah neh yeem _____
meat	mjasa	MYAH-sah
chicken	kurki	KOORR-kih
fish	ribi	RRIH-bih
eggs	jajets	yai-YEHTS

cheese	siru	SIHR-roo
I eat ____ and ____.	Ja yim ____ i ____.	yah yeem ____ ee ____
meat	mjaso	MYAH-soh
chicken	kurku	KOOR-koo
fish	ribu	RRIH-boo
eggs	jajtse	yai-TSEH
cheese	sir	seer
I am a vegetarian. *(male speaker)*	Ja vegetarianets´.	yah veh-heh-tah-ree-AH-nehtz
I am a vegetarian. *(female speaker)*	Ja vegetarianka.	yah veh-heh-tah-ree-AHN-kah
Please.	Prošu.	PROH-shoo
Thank you.	Djakyu.	DYAH-koo-yoo

chapter four
NORTH AFRICA AND THE MIDDLE EAST

North Africa and the Middle East share the salient char-
acteristic of being overwhelmingly arid or semi-arid.
This factor influences the cuisine of the region in myriad ways.
For example, beef and pork are mostly absent—beef for climatic and
economic reasons, pork because the region is mainly Muslim.
Instead, lamb and goat are the most common meats. For vegetarians,
this simply means there are generally fewer types of meat to
avoid. Similarly, dairy products are not as prevalent as in North
America or Europe, although yogurt and goat or sheep (or in some
places, camel) milk and cheese are fairly common. The climate also
limits the range of crops. Certain kinds of grains, such as wheat
or millet, a small grain commonly found here, along with legumes
like lentils, chickpeas, and kidney beans, form the basis of the
diet. Nuts, fruits, and vegetables round out the offerings, particularly in irrigated areas. In many countries throughout the region
it is easy to find meatless dishes centered on these basic ingredients.

There can be substantial variations between countries, however.

In some countries the average diet is quite spartan, while in others meat (or fish) in some form almost always accompanies—or smothers—meatless portions. Nonetheless, it is usually possible to find something edible and meatless. Guests may have special difficulties: Arab hospitality is legendary, and a visitor may be served a mighty selection of dishes, including some highly unappetizing animal portions. You may be expected to sample (although not necessarily to finish) everything that is placed before you. Not doing so would cause great offense. The only respectable alternative might be to feign a severe allergy (which should not be too difficult with a sheep's eye staring at you).

The dominant language of the region is **Arabic**. Spoken Arabic varies dramatically from one region to another; the Arabic spoken in Morocco will be very different in many respects from the Arabic spoken in Yemen, for example. Nonetheless, the phrases listed below are fairly simple and should be understood by Arabic-speakers throughout North Africa and the Middle East. The local pronunciation may be different, but you will probably sound merely stilted and strange, not totally incomprehensible.

Arabic

The phrases below have been transliterated from the ornate script used to write Arabic.

I would like something without _____.	Ana orid akil biduun _____.	ah-NAH ow-REED AH-keel bee-doon _____
We would like something without _____.	Ehna norid akil biduun _____.	eh-NAH now-REED AH-keel bee-doon _____
I do not eat _____.	Ana la akoul _____.	ah-NAH lah AH-kool _____

I eat ____	Ana akoul ____	ah-NAH AH-kool
and ____ .	wa ____ .	____ wah ____
meat	laham	lah-KHAM
chicken	dajaj	dah-zhahzh
fish	samak	sah-mahk
eggs	baid	byde
cheese	joubnah	zhihbb-nah
Please.	Min fadlak.	meen FAHD-lahk
or	Raja'an.	rah-zhah-ahn
Thank you.	Shukran.	shuh-KRAHN

A. North Africa

The countries along the southern rim of the Mediterranean Sea bask in a beneficent climate, and produce wonderful fruits and vegetables. However, most North Africans have a rather basic diet, the exact substance of which changes as one moves from west to east. *Couscous*, a crushed semolina dish, is the staple food in the Maghreb (Morocco, Algeria, and Tunisia). Egypt is more cosmopolitan, with notable Middle Eastern influences. Vegetarianism is not really practiced much in this area, and most North Africans gladly eat meat when they can get it. Nonetheless, it should be possible to avoid meat in all but the most remote desert areas.

Algeria

Algerian food is similar to that of its neighbors, Morocco and Tunisia: *Couscous* is the staple, and meat takes on a supporting role as soup and sauce ingredient. Some vegetable or lentil-based dishes are available, mainly in the form of side dishes or appetizers; one common example is *makouda*, made with eggs, potatoes, parsley, and lentils. Vegetable stews are quite common, but these are usually made with meat stock. In the Sahara, vegetables become less common (understandably so!); couscous is usually available, however. European-style restaurants are scattered throught the cities of the north; these often offer at least one meatless entree, such as pizza or spaghetti.

Arabic (p. 112) is the official language. Berber dialects are also spoken. Many Algerians speak French as a second language.

Egypt

It is a heartening sign that the Egyptian national dish is *fuul*—fava or kidney beans in a spicy sauce. Although lamb and other fleshy items such as goose are very popular, there is a decent variety of meatless food available. Eggplant dishes, rice with nuts and dried fruit, and Lebanese-style food such as *falafel*, *baba ghanoush*, and *hummus* are all common. Another often-available dish, stuffed grape leaves, is occasionally filled with rice and lentils insetad of meat. Typical snack foods include *sambousek* (pastries filled with cheese or vegetables) and *fiteer* (a cross between a pastry and pizza, filled with meat, eggs, or white cheese). Some varieties of vegetable or legume soups do not contain meat (although they are sometimes made with meat stock).

In Cairo and Alexandria, and to a lesser extent in smaller cities and tourist centers, there are plenty of Indian restaurants and restaurants serving European-style food such as pasta.

Arabic (p. 112) is the official language. People who deal with tourists can usually speak English or French (or both).

Libya

Libya is at the crossroads of North Africa, and its food reflects its geographical position. The *fuul* (kidney or fava beans) of Egypt is in evidence, while the *couscous* of the Maghreb countries is also very popular. Unfortunately, Libyan *couscous* is sometimes cooked in lamb stock, and is often served with meat sauce. There are some vegetable stews, but these usually have a meat base, or else have unappetizing chunks of lamb or mutton floating in them. A third culinary influence—that of the Italians who colonized and occupied Libya—is apparent in the various permutations of pasta that are widely available.

Arabic (p. 112) is the national language. Italian can be useful, especially with older Libyans, but its use is decreasing as a policy of Arabicization takes hold.

Morocco

Morocco is best known for *couscous,* a dish of semolina or other grains made into small, pasta-like pieces. While *couscous* may be a vegetarian's lifesaver in Morocco, it can be hard to find in restaurants as it is usually eaten at home, and is at its best when homemade. Even when *couscous* is available, it is often covered in meat sauce; Moroccans tend to make use of as much meat as they can. Another famous Moroccan dish, *tajine* (a kind of stew) usually contains lamb or other meat, but is occasionally meat-free. Other types of soup are frequently made with lamb stock, even if actual chunks of meat are absent. *Harira* (lentil stew) is often meatless. Meatless sandwiches are easy to find. In towns, French-style bakeries, restaurants, and cafes offer another option, although apart from bread, pastries, and sandwiches, the range of meatless offerings can be slim. Good yogurt is easily available in shops and fruit, especially citrus fruit, is ubiquitous.

Arabic (p. 112) is the official language. Berber dialects are spoken in the mountains and in the interior. French is commonly spoken as a second language. Spanish is useful in the far north. Moroccans who deal regularly with tourists are amazing linguists, and are sometimes proficient in 7 or 8 languages (including English).

Western Sahara, a former Spanish colony, is now under *de facto* Moroccan control. The diet is considerably less varied than in Morocco proper; couscous, fish, and meat are the most common foods. While Arabic is the most common language here, Spanish (p. 70) remains useful.

Tunisia

Of the Maghreb region cuisines, Tunisian food displays the most European influence. French bread (plain or stuffed) is served all over Tunisia, and the cities have many French-style cafes and restaurants. Many European-style restaurants serve one or two meatless dishes. Pasta and pizza are extremely common. Because meat is so expensive, the basic diet of most Tunisians consists of grains and legumes, with vegetables or fruit; meat is used only in small amounts. However, Tunisians eat meat with gusto on special occasions, such as at restaurant meals or when a guest is present. Couscous, the Tunisian staple, is available in many varieties, but is often served with meat sauce. Salads, roasted or fried vegetables, and lentil or vegetable soups, are all fairly common. Tunisian fruit is outstanding. Along the coast, fish is devoured by all and sundry (except for vegetarians). Several common snack items may be suitable for vegetarians; these include spinach and vegetable turnovers, *briq* (an egg-filled pastry), and *chaksuka* (chopped vegetables and egg). However, these sometimes contain bits of meat.

Arabic (p. 112) is the official language. Most Tunisians can also speak French.

B. The Middle East

Several dishes that many vegetarians know and love trace their origins to the Middle East. They include *hummus* (a chickpea-based dip), tabouli (a cracked-wheat and vegetable salad), and *falafel* (fried balls of spiced chickpea flour). While these dishes are common in many Middle Eastern countries, the cuisine of the region can be much richer and more complex (and in many cases, less vegetarian-friendly). Some countries in the region, particularly Turkey and the Caucasus nations (Armenia, Georgia, and Azerbaijan), have unique cuisines that are very different from what is normally thought of as Middle Eastern cooking. The countries of the Arabian peninsula place the most importance on meat, and the food can be unrelentingly monotonous. In most cases, though, a vegetarian in the Middle East should be able to find something tasty and meat-free to eat, if only an assortment of appetizers or side dishes.

Armenia

Armenia offers an impressive variety of imaginative vegetarian options. Although few Armenians are full-time vegetarians, most people give up meat, and sometimes all animal products, during Lent and other times of fasting. The dishes crafted to cope with forced meatless periods are so good that they are often available throughout the year. Potential ingredients include bulgur, rice, eggplant, chickpeas, and a bountiful array of fruits, vegetables, and nuts. Most dishes are served with a sauce that is based on olive-oil or tomato; sometimes the sauce contains dried fruits, almonds, or pine nuts. Omelettes, sheep cheese, flat bread or yeast bread, *boeregs* (turnovers), and a host of *meza* (appetizers) all provide excellent meatless sustenance. One should not forget that many Armenian dishes do contain meat, so ordering at random from a menu is not recommended. Still, Armenia remains a relatively easy country for meat-free eating.

Armenian is the national language. Russian (p. 99) can also be useful.

Armenian

The words and pharases below have been transliterated from Armenian script.

I do not eat ____.	Yes chemm ooder ____.	yehss chehm oo-DEHR ____
I eat ____.	Yes goodem ____.	yehss goo-DEHM ____
meat	mis	mees
chicken	hav	hahv
fish	dzouk	tsoog
eggs	havkit	hahv-KEET
cheese	baneer	bah-NEER
I am a vegetarian.	Pancharager em.	pahn-chah-rah-GEHR ehm
Please.	Hajees.	hah-jees
Thank you.	Shnoragalem.	shuh-nohr-ah-GAH-lehm

Azerbaijan

Unlike its mostly Orthodox Christian neighbors Georgia and Armenia, Azerbaijan is a predominantly Muslim country, and thus lacks the meatless fasting periods that have given rise to the wide variety of vegetarian dishes in those countries. However, with some effort, it is perfectly possible to avoid meat. Azerbaijan is the home of rice pilaf and, while this is often served with sides of lamb or other meat, you are certainly under no compulsion to eat the meat. (Pilaf is sometimes made with stock, however.) Azerbaijanis make good use of dried fruit and nuts, so pilafs are usually more than just seasoned rice. There are also many meatless appetizers that can be combined to make a full meal.

Azeri is the national tongue. Russian can be helpful. Armenian (p. 117) is spoken by a small minority of the population.

Azeri

I would like something without ____.	Mən ____ bir shey yemək istərdim.	mahn ____ beer shay yeh-MAHK ee-stahr-deem
meat	ətsiz	aht-SEEZ
chicken	toyugsuz	toy-ookh-SOOZ
fish	balygsyz	bah-lihkh-SIHZ
eggs	yumurtasyz	yoo-moor-tah-SIHZ
cheese	pendirsiz	pehn-deer-SIHZ
I do not eat ____.	Mən ____ yemirəm.	mahn ____ yeh-MEER-ahm
I eat ____ and ____.	Mən ____ ve yeyirəm.	mahn ____ vah ____ yeh-YEER-ahm
meat	ət	aht
chicken	toyugət	toy-oog-aht
fish	balyg	bah-lihg

eggs	yumurta	yoo-moor-TAH
cheese	pendir	pehn-DEER
Please.	Buyurun.	boy-yoo-roon
Thank you.	Chokh sag olun.	chohkh sahkh oh-LOON

Bahrain

Bahrain offers the standard cuisine of the Gulf region—which is to say it offers little in the way of culinary enticement to vegetarians. Rice and meat form the centerpiece of the Bahraini diet. However, Lebanese-style food such as *falafel* is fairly common. The presence of many foreign workers in Bahrain ensures that there is a fair selection of Asian cuisine: Indian, Pakistani, Thai, Filipino, and Chinese restaurants are present. As a final option, Western-style restaurants or hotel restaurants usually can rustle up a meatless dish.

Arabic (p. 112) is the main language. Other West Asian languages such as Farsi and Urdu are spoken by foreign workers. English is a common second language.

Cyprus

Cyprus is currently riven into two parts. The northern half is occupied by Turkish troops and considers itself an independent country. (Most of the rest of the world disagrees.) The southern half of the island is mainly inhabited by ethnic Greeks. As a result of this sharp division, travelers will find that food in the north is much like food in Turkey, while food in the unoccupied zone strongly resembles Greek food in many ways. Due to its geographical location, there is also a strong Middle Eastern influence throughout the island (pita bread and *hummus* is widely available, for example).

Although Cypriots enjoy meat and fish, it is not difficult for vegetarians to eat well in Cyprus. During Lent, Eastern Orthodox Cypriots avoid meat, fish, and dairy products, and many dishes are designed to be served at this time. The rest of the year, tavernas offer a wide selection of *meze* (appetizers), many of which are flesh-free. There are also an excellent variety of meatless soups and main dishes, which may contain beans or lentils, cracked wheat, yogurt, eggplant, greens, or rice.

Cyprus is linguistically divided along the same lines as its political and gastronomic divisions. Most people in northern Cyprus speak **Turkish** (p. 131); the more numerous southern Cypriots speak **Greek** (p. 62). Cyprus was formerly administered by Britain, so English is also widely spoken as a second language.

Georgia

Many Georgians look down on vegetarianism as something of an effete and undesirable habit. Nonetheless, while vegetarianism *per se* is not practiced widely in Georgia, the country has an astounding variety of meatless dishes. Many of these dishes were developed to cope with the lengthy meatless religious fasts of the Georgian Orthodox church, but they are usually available throughout the year. Eggplant is one of the most common dishes, and is served in many forms. *Lobio* (bean-based dishes) are also very available but sometimes are made with stock. Grains or vegetables are usually served with a sauce which sometimes contain meat but are often made with garlic, herbs, yogurt, or nuts (especially walnuts). *Khachapuri* (bread filled with cheese) is a common snack. Georgia's fertile soil and good climate ensure that vegetables, fruit, and nuts are widely available and widely used (fruit is dried for use throughout the year). Dairy products are also very common; most cheese is made from sheep or goat milk, and Georgian yogurt is outstanding. (Its consumption is widely believed to be the reason for the longevity of the centenarians who inhabit the mountains).

Georgian (not the drawl heard in Atlanta) is the official language. Russian (p. 99) and Armenian (p.117) are spoken by small minorities.

Georgian

The words below have been transliterated from Georgian script.

I would like something without _____.	Tu sheydzleba, rame _____.	too SHAYDS-lay-bah, RAH-may _____
meat	u xortsod	oo KHOHRT-sohd
chicken	katmis xortsis gareshe	kaht-mees KHOHRT-sees GAH-ray-shay
fish	utevzod	OO-tehv-zohd
eggs	kvertsxis gareshe	kvehr-EHTS-khees GAH-ray shay
cheese	uxvelod	OOKH-vay-lohd
I do not eat _____.	Arvcham _____.	AHRV-chahm _____
I eat _____ and _____.	Meh vcham _____ da _____.	mayv chahm _____ dah _____
meat	xorts	khohrts
chicken	katmis xorts	kaht-mees khohrts

122

fish	tevz	tayvz
eggs	kvertsks	kVAYRTSks
cheese	kvels	kvayls
Thank you.	Madlobt.	MAHD-lohbt

Iran

Visitors who are allowed into the country will find that the basic staple is rice, served either plain or mixed with fruit, meat, or vegetables. Rice pilaf is a common dish, but it is usually made with meat stock. Salads are generally available but, apart from rice dishes, the order of the day is *kebabs*—not good news for vegetarians. There are some interesting meatless Iranian soups, such as yogurt or fruit soups, but these can be difficult to find. Near the Gulf and along the Caspian Sea, pesco-vegetarians will find plenty of fish. There are a few Western-style or Indian restaurants in the cities (although the number of the former has understandably decreased since the Islamic revolution).

Farsi (Persian) is the predominant language, and is spoken in an array of dialects. Farsi-derived Dari (p. 203) and Tajik (p. 208) are used in the northeast. Kurdish (p. 125) is spoken in the far northwest. Turkic languages such as Azeri (p. 119) and Turkmen (p. 209) are spoken in some places in the far north and east.

Farsi

The words and phrases below have been transliterated from the Persian alphabet.

I would like something without ____.	Man yek chizy bedane ____ mikhaham.	mahn yehk CHEE-zee beh-doh-nay ____ mee-KHAH-hahm

I do not eat ____.	Man ____ nemikhoram.	mahn ____ nay-mee-**kh**oh-rahm
I eat ____ and ____.	Man ____ va ____ mikhoram.	mahn ____ vah ____ mee-**kh**oh-rahm
meat	gosht	goosht
chicken	morgh	mohrk
fish	mahi	mah-hee
eggs	tokhme-morgh	to**kh**-may-mohrk
cheese	paneer	pah-NEER
I am a vegetarian.	Man sabzeekar has-tam.	mahn sahb-zee-kahr hah-STAHM
Please.	Lotfan.	loht-FAHN
Thank you.	Mersy.	mehrr-SEE
or	Mamnoon.	mahm-NOON

Iraq

Iraqi food is not particularly distinguished. Traditionally, meat has been a major ingredient in Iraqi cooking, although the United Nations embargo cut into its dominance by making meat quite expensive. Many meatless foods of Lebanese origin, such as *falafel*, *hummus*, *tabouli*, and *baba ghanoush*, are on offer. These are generally served with thin Iraqi-style pita bread or French bread, and are the most accessible and widely available meatless options. Rice dishes are common but these are often cooked in stock. Assorted vegetable or legume soups and stews make appearances, but again, these often contain meat stock or bits of meat. Iraqi-style pizza is also available.

Arabic (p. 112) is the official language. **Kurdish** is spoken in the north.

Kurdish

I do not eat _____.	Ez _____ na xwem.	ahz _____ nah KHWAHM
I eat _____ and _____.	Ez _____ û _____ dixwem.	ahz _____ oouh _____ teh-KHWAHM
meat	gosht	goosht
chicken	mirishk	meh-REHSHK
fish	masi	mah-seh
eggs	heq	hahk
cheese	penir	pah-NEHR
Please.	Lotfen.	loht-FAHN
Thank you.	Spas.	spahz

Israel and Palestine

Vegetarians will find it reasonably easy to find suitable sustenance in Israel and Palestine. There are a number of specialty vegetarian restaurants in Israel, although it is rarely necessary to resort to them. Lacto-vegetarians will be pleased at the number of dairy restaurants in Israel; orthodox Judaism forbids the consumption of milk and meat at the same time, and this proscription has led to a proliferation of Kosher dairy restaurants that serve no meat or fish at all. Ordinary restaurants often offer meatless dishes, especially salads and prepared vegetables such as eggplant. Many soups are made with meat stock, however. Because Israel has seen so much immigration, cuisines from all over the world are represented, and provide an interesting change of pace.

The most popular fast-food throughout Israel and Palestine is *falafel*, which is sold at stands, shops, and restaurants everywhere. It is served in pita bread, often covered in *tahini* (sesame paste). Roasted corn-on-the-cob and *bourekas*, flaky pastries with a (usually) meatless cheese or vegetable filling, are also common snacks. Those who cook for themselves will find a wonderful variety of fruits and vegetables available, as well as good yogurt and other dairy products. The word *"pareve"* on packaging means that the food within was prepared without milk or meat.

The food in Palestinian areas does not differ dramatically from that in Israel itself, although Kosher restaurants are understandably absent. *Hummus, falafel,* and *fuul* (kidney or fava beans) are popular, and many common *mazza* (appetizers) are meatless. Spinach pastries are filling, cheap, and ubiquitous.

Hebrew and **Arabic** (p. 112) are the official languages of Israel. Hebrew is the predominant tongue in Israel proper; Arabic is the main language in Palestinian areas of Gaza and the West Bank. English is widely spoken in Israel.

Hebrew

Hebrew has its own alphabet, and is read from right to left. In the following words and phrases, Hebrew characters have been transliterated into the Roman alphabet.

I would like something without _____.	Ani avakesh mashehoo bli _____.	ah-NEE ah-vah-KEHSH mah-sheh-HOO blee _____
We would like something without _____.	Anachnu nevakesh mashehoo bli _____.	ah-NAHKH-noo neh-vah-KEHSH mah-sheh-HOO blee _____
I do not eat _____. *(male speaker)*	Ani lo ochel _____.	ah-NEE loh OH-khehl _____
I do not eat _____. *(female speaker)*	Ani lo ochelet _____.	ah-NEE loh OH-khehl-eht _____
I eat _____ and _____.	Ani ochel _____ ve _____.	ah-NEE OH-khehl _____ vay _____
meat	basar	bah-SAHL
chicken	of	ohff
fish	dag	dahg
eggs	beizim	bay-TZEEM
cheese	gvina	GVEE-nah
I am a vegetarian. *(male speaker)*	Ani tzimchoni.	ah-NEE tseem-KHOH-nee

I am a vegetarian. *(female speaker)*	Ani tzimchonit.	ah-NEE tseem-KHOH-neet
Please.	Bevakasha.	beh-vah-kah-SHAH
Thank you.	Toda.	toh-DAH

Jordan

Jordanian food borrows heavily from Lebanese influences. While lamb is a favorite meal, *hummus*, *tabouli*, and the usual suspects are available in abundance. *Falafel* stands are as common in Jordan as hamburger joints are in North America. A Jordanian version of pizza is also fairly common (and very tasty). Several common appetizers and main dishes are meat- free, such as eggplant and rice, various salads, and *fuul* (kidney beans). There are also Western and Asian restaurants in the cities.

Arabic (p. 112) is the official language.

Kuwait

Beware the warm Kuwati welcome: guests are often welcomed with the slaughter of a sheep! As one might imagine from this custom, meatless dishes do not abound in Kuwait. Rice with meat or fish is the rule, sometimes accompanied by vegetables stuffed with meat. *Fuul* (kidney beans) is common, however. The best choice for vegetarians in Kuwait is probably to take refuge in one of the many Chinese or Indian restaurants. There are a number of American-style fast-food restaurants (with all that that implies for vegetarians). There are also a few Lebanese restaurants that serve *falafel*.

Arabic (p. 112) is the official language.

Lebanon

Most of what is commonly thought of as typical Middle Eastern food—*hummus*, *falafel*, *tabouli*, *baba ghanoush* (eggplant dip) and the like—is of Lebanese origin. While lamb, chicken, and fish all have their day in Lebanese kitchens, there are plenty of meatless dishes to choose from, in addition to the stereotypical ones listed above. Lebanon is one of the most fertile countries of the Middle East, and the fruits and vegetables it produces are put to good use in Lebanese dishes. Most produce is fresh and local; eggplant, spinach, and other vegetable dishes are commonplace. It is easy to find salads or appetizers served with pita bread and based on grains, greens, or beans such as *fuul* (kidney beans). Lebanese potato salad does not contain eggs.

Arabic (p. 112) and **French** (p. 60) are both official languages. Arabic is more useful, as it is the first language of most Lebanese.

Oman

The typical Omani diet, like the diet of most Gulf countries, is based on rice and fish or lamb (although Omanis tend to spice their food up somewhat more than their neighbors to the north do). However, most restaurants serve some kind of meatless entree; there are even a few vegetarian specialty restaurants (a rarity in the Gulf region). In addition to the many Chinese, Indian, and southeast Asian restaurants, there is a contingent of Western-style restaurants whose offerings range from bland "international" cuisine to pizza and pasta.

Arabic (p. 112) is the official language.

Qatar

The Qatari diet generally consists of rice with meat or fish. Such a diet obviously holds few attractions for the visiting vegetarian. Fortunately, Indians and Pakistanis make up over one third of Qatar's population. As one would expect, Indian restaurants are common, and are probably the best and most accessible option for meatless dishes (although many of the dishes in these restaurants do contain meat). Western-style restaurants exist, and may be a good option for salads or other meatless dishes.

Arabic (p. 112) is the official language. Other West Asian languages and English are also spoken.

Saudi Arabia

Saudi Arabia is the home of a vegetarian's nightmare: the so-called "goat grab," a meal of a whole roast sheep or goat. Such meals are often prepared to welcome visitors, so a vegetarian who is welcomed in this fashion is in a quandary indeed. Apart from these flesh fests, Saudi Arabia can be culinarily manageable. The average Saudi eats lots of rice, although usually with chicken, fish, or lamb. You are free to eat only the rice, although this diet may grow tiresome. *Fuul* (kidney beans) and *samosas* are very common (although the latter often contain meat). Salads and fruit (both fresh and dried) are easy to find. Adventurous non-vegans can try camel milk and cheese. In the cities, Indian, Chinese and other restaurants offer vegetarian dishes. There are also many Western-style restaurants in urban areas, which sometimes serve meatless food such as pizza or pasta. In the Saudi desert, among the Bedouin, you should probably be prepared to eat meat or go hungry. As a compromise between these extremes, it might be best to bring your own provisions (be prepared to share).

Arabic (p. 112) is the principal language. English is often spoken in the cities.

Syria

Syrian food is a blend of influences from Turkey, Lebanon, Armenia, and elsewhere in the Middle East. While meat dishes such as *kebab* or *kibby* (a ground beef mixture) are everywhere, there are plenty of meatless options from which to choose. As in neighboring Lebanon, *hummus*, *falafel*, and pita bread are common offerings. There are many vegetarian side dishes and main dishes, such as eggplant (served hot or cold), squash with yogurt sauce, eggless potato salad, or bean salads. Cracked wheat is often served in salad or in other forms.

Arabic (p. 112) is the official language. Kurdish (p. 125) is spoken in parts of the northeast; Armenian (p. 117) is spoken by a very small minority.

Turkey

Turkish cuisine is much more than the stereotypical skewer of shishkebab. In fact, while lamb and other meats are very common and often served in the form of *kebab*, there are many options for vegetarians. The most promising dishes are known as *zeytinyagli* (zeh-tin-yah-lee), which are made with olive oil and lots of vegetables. *Zeytinyagli* are served cold, usually as *mezze* (appetizers) or side dishes, and are even available in most kebab houses. Be careful in the hinterlands of central and eastern Turkey—cooks may occasionally throw in pieces of meat.

Besides *zeytinyagli*, many side and main dishes are meat-free. Greek-style salads with feta and olives are common; *ali nazik* is an eggplant, cheese, and yogurt concoction; *biber dolmasi* contains rice, tomatoes, and spices. *Börek* are savory pastries containing vegetables or cheese (and sometimes meat). Various other dishes are made with a tomato-onion base and contain no meat. However, soups and some cooked bean or vegetable dishes sometimes contain meat stock. Turkish pizza and the bagel-like *simit* make good snacks.

The description above mostly applies to western and, to a lesser extent, central Turkey. In eastern Turkey, entirely vegetarian dishes may be difficult to find; mutton and goat form the basis of the diet and in some cases there may be little else to eat. Pesco-vegetarians should note that fish is served everywhere along the coast.

Turkish is the official national language. Kurdish (p. 125) dialects are spoken in the southeast.

Turkish

I would like something without ____.	____ birsey istiyorum.	____ beer-SHAY ees-TEE-yoh-room

We would like something without ____.	____ birseyler istiyoruz.	____ beer-shay-LEHR ees-TEE-yoh-rooz
meat	etsiz	eht-SEEZ
chicken	tavuksuz	tah-vook-SOOZ
fish	balıksız	bah-luhk-SUHZ
eggs	yumurtasız	yoo-moor-tah-SUHZ
cheese	peynirsiz	pay-neer-SEEZ
I do not eat ____.	____ yemem.	____ yeh-MAHM
I eat ____ and ____.	____ ve ____ yerim.	____ veh ____ YEH-reem
meat	et	eht
chicken	tavuk	tah-VOOK
fish	balık	bah-LUHK
eggs	yumurta	yoo-moor-TAH
cheese	peynir	pay-NEER
I am a vegetarian.	Ben vejeteryenim	behn veh-zheh-tehr-YEHN- eem

Please	Lutfen.	LOOT-fahn
Thank you.	Tesekkurler.	teh-shehk-koor-LEHR

United Arab Emirates

These Emirates are united, among other ways, in their fairly bland diet of rice eaten with meat or fish. However, there are many Western-style restaurants that offer pizza, pasta, salads, and other meatless dishes. Many different Asian cuisines are also represented here; Chinese and Indian/Pakistani restaurants are particularly common. Lebanese-style food (*falafel* and *hummus*) is available.

Arabic (p. 112) is the official language. Due to the presence of many foreign workers in the U.A.E., many Asian languages, as well as English, are spoken.

Yemen

Yemenis are not heavy meat eaters, but they are hardly intentional vegetarians, either. The standard diet is grains, bread, or beans, usually served with fish or meat sauce or soup. Most soups have meat or are made with meat stock, but there are some meatless vegetable or yogurt soups that can occasionally be found in local restaurants. A variety of vegetables are eaten as side dishes. *Fuul* (kidney beans) is a common dish, as is *salta* (mixed vegetables with a spicy mustard sauce). Rice is the most common grain, but potatoes and sorghum are also eaten. There are a few western-style restaurants serving pasta and the like. As a last resort, one can chew *qat*, a widely-used stimulant and appetite suppressant.

Arabic (p. 112) is the main language of Yemen.

chapter five
AFRICA
SOUTH OF THE SAHARA

A frica is a vast continent with substantial regional differences in culture, language, and geography. The cuisine of sub-Saharan Africa, however, is not as diverse as that of some other areas of the world, partly because of limited indigenous ingredients and partly because of general poverty. In most areas of the continent, some sort of starch—rice, cornmeal, millet, or tubers such as yam or cassava—forms the basis of the diet. The starch is generally supplemented by soups, sauces, or stews, which typically contain meat or fish (although they are sometimes vegetable-based). Exact ingredients vary from country to country. The availability of fresh fruit and vegetables also varies wildly. European-style food is common in many urban or resort areas, although all too often it is merely some version of the worst of neo-colonial cuisine: greasy french fries, steak or hamburger, or some other unhealthy concoction. Indian or Middle Eastern food can be found in many countries.

Throughout most of Africa, cheese is a foreign concept. In

most countries, there is no indigenous word for cheese, and the word from the relevant colonial language is used (e.g., *fromage* in former French colonies).

Thousands of languages are spoken in Africa, most of which are very limited in geographical range. The prevalence of minor tribal languages, combined with the arbitrary nature of colonial boundaries, means that most African countries have no universal indigenous language. (Conversely, some African languages are spoken in more than one country.) The official language of most countries is the European language of the relevant former colonial power. However, in many countries, not everyone can speak the official language; people who are used to dealing with tourists or who have been formally educated usually can. In some countries, an indigenous language has become the *de facto* tongue of inter-ethnic communication.

The most useful regional languages are Hausa (p. 145), Bambara-Dioula (p. 142), and Wolof (p. 149) in West Africa; Swahili (p. 157) in East Africa; and Afrikaans (p. 180) in parts of southern Africa.

A. West Africa

While the quality of West African food varies from one country to another, the basic substance is the same throughout much of the region. The standard meal is starch with sauce or soup, sometimes accompanied by vegetables and greens. The starch is usually rice, millet, or some form of cassava, banana, yam, or sweet potato. The sauces are often marvelous, frequently based on vegetables or peanuts. However, even vegetable or nut sauces sometimes contain meat or fish; fish is the most common additive along the coast or near major rivers, while chicken or lamb are used in inland areas. Okra and other vegetables, or greens such as cassava leaves, are served as side dishes. Western food is available in almost all countries, and is usually most prevalent in urban areas.

Benin

Beninese food fits the standard West African model: starch (usually rice, cassava, or yam) with sauce or stew. Sauces in Benin tend to display more flair than those in some other countries in the region. Unfortunately, these sauces usually contain meat, although there are a few purely vegetarian sauces, typically based on okra or spinach-like greens. Meatless peanut sauce is sometimes available. Pesco-vegetarians will be happy to know that fish is available everywhere along the coast, and along rivers in inland areas; sardines with tomatoes is a common dish. Cotonou has a few European-style restaurants that serve pizza, pasta, French bread, and other accoutrements of neo-colonialism.

French (p. 60) is the official language. In the south, Yoruba (p. 147) is common. Various tribal languages are spoken in the north.

Burkina Faso

Burkina Faso is a fascinating but poor country with an equally poor selection of vegetarian food. Most restaurants, such as they are, concentrate on grilled meat or fish and are neither particularly representative of Burkinan food nor very amenable to vegetarianism. Food stalls are a better (if less sanitary) bet for vegetarians. The core of the diet of most "Burkinabae" is millet or rice with sauce. Most homemade sauces are vegetarian (due to the cost of meat), but stall-bought sauces may contain some meat. Stews such as yam stew and okra stew are common, as are plain greens and sweet potatoes. European-style restaurants, bakeries, and creameries in Ouagadougou and Bobo Dioulasso provide a welcome break from food stands.

French (p. 60) is the official language. The main market language is Bambara-Dioula (p.142). Many other indigenous languages are spoken, including Hausa (p. 145) and Pulaar (p. 143).

Cape Verde

The Cape Verde archipelago is bathed in the waters of the

tropical Atlantic, so, naturally, fish is the mainstay of the diet. Pesco-vegetarians should have a field day, but stricter vegetarians will run into problems. (Chicken is fairly popular, but it is hardly a viable vegetarian alternative.) Rice is the staple starch, and is sometimes eaten with beans; fried bananas make up a typical side dish. Turnovers and other pastry-type dishes are common snacks, but they often contain fish or meat.

Portuguese (p. 67) is the official language, and is widely spoken. The main everyday language is **Crioulo,** a mixture of Portuguese and African dialects.

Crioulo

I do not eat _____.	Um ka pode come _____.	oom kah pohd koh-may _____
meat	carne	kahrn
chicken	galinha	gah-leen-yah
fish	peixe	paysh
eggs	of	ohf
Thank you. *(female speaker)*	Obrigada.	oh-bree-GAH-dah
Thank you. *(male speaker)*	Obrigado.	oh-bree-GAH-doh

Côte d'Ivoire

Ivoirien cuisine tends to follow the starch-and-sauce model of other West African countries. The starches include *foutou* (pounded, pasta-like starchy cakes) made from cassava, yam, plaintain, or banana, rice, or *attieke* (grated cassava) made into a sort of couscous. Generally, the starches are served with sauces made with chicken, fish, or occasionally beef; however, it is sometimes possible to get vegetable sauces. Food stalls often sell snacks such as bananas or plantains, grilled and mashed or fried in palm oil. The cities of Côte d'Ivoire have more European restaurants than most other West African countries do, and French, Italian, and other cuisines are available. There are even a few Chinese and Middle Eastern restaurants in Abidjan.

French (p. 60) is the official language. Of the 60-plus native dialects, Bambara-Dioula (p. 142) is the most common, and is used as a market language everywhere.

The Gambia

The Gambia is a long, skinny country strung along the river of the same name that is the lifeblood of the country, and fish is correspondingly important in the Gambian diet. Rice, millet, and mashed cassava or yam are all widely-used starches. These are usually served with stews that are sometimes vegetarian, but are often made with fish or chicken. (For example, peanut stew is common, but frequently contains chicken.) Restaurants tend to concentrate on chicken and fish dishes. French fries and other unhealthy Western snack foods are easily available.

English is the official language; several indigenous languages are spoken in The Gambia. Wolof (p. 149) is the most common indigenous language along the coast. In the interior, there are speakers of Bambara-Dioula (p. 142), Pulaar (p. 143), and Mandinka, as well as several other tongues.

Mandinka

I do not eat ____.	Mbu ka ____ domo.	mBOO kah ____ doh-moh
meat	subo	soo-boh
chicken	sousse	soo-say

fish	ñie	nyeh
eggs	sousse kilo	soo-say kee-loh
Thank you.	Abaraka.	ah-bah-RAH-kah

Ghana

Along with the standard West African starches—rice, cassava, millet, yam, plaintain, and corn—Ghanians created some wonderful sauces. Sadly, most of these sauces, including the archetypal peanut sauce, are usually made with chicken or fish. With some diligent searching (or a pleasant manner), it is often possible to find vegetable sauces or stews made with pumpkin or other squashes, spinach, okra, or eggplant. Fried sweet potato is a common snack food, as are cornmeal balls and fried plantains. In Accra and to a lesser extent in cities throughout the country, Western-style food is reasonably common, but not necessarily helpful to vegetarians. (For example, fish and chips is popular, reflecting Ghana's British colonial history.) There are a few Indian, Middle Eastern, and assorted other seemingly misplaced eateries in the cities.

English is the official language. Nearly half the population speaks **Twi**. Some Hausa (p. 145) is spoken in the north, while Ewe (p. 151) is spoken in the southeast.

Twi

I do not eat _____.	Mi ndi ____.	meen-DEE ____
meat *(this word also encompasses fish)*	nam	nahm
chicken	akoko	ah-koh-koh

140

eggs	kosier	KOH-see-ehrr
Thank you.	Medasi.	may-DAH-see

Guinea

In common with its neighbors, rice or other starches with sauce is the standard Guinean meal. Usually the sauce contains fish or occasionally chicken, but vegetarian varieties are sometimes available. Fried bananas are a common snack, and other fruits such as pineapple are common. There are a few Western restaurants in Conakry, including some French cafes; outside Conakry, there is very little variation in available food.

French (p. 60) is the official language. Many indigenous languages are spoken in the interior, including Pulaar (p. 143).

Guinea-Bissau

The cuisine of Guinea-Bissau is not particularly distinguished. Fish is a staple, and rice, yam, and cassava are the usual starches. Fried bananas are a common snack. There are some decent Western-style restaurants in the capital, which may be good sources for welcome, if unimaginative, meatless food.

Portuguese (p. 67) is the official language. The lingua franca is Crioulo (p. 138). Wolof (p. 149), Mandinka (p. 139) and other indigenous languages are also spoken.

Liberia

Liberia's unfortunate recent history of civil war and famine means that there is very little variety to the average Liberian's diet. Cassava, rice, and sweet potatoes are the most common starches. These are traditionally topped with a sauce or stew, and served with greens such as cassava leaves or okra. With luck, the sauce will be vegetarian—meat is difficult to come by during times of privation and dislocation. Hopefully, peace will be maintained, and a greater variety of food will be available both for the local population and for the traveler.

English is the official language, and the small minority of Liberians who are of African-American descent speak it as a mother tongue. More than two dozen local languages are spoken in Liberia.

Mali

Mali is a dry, dusty (albeit historically fascinating) country with relatively little variety in its cuisine. "Couscous" (made from millet) and rice are the staple starches. Soups, stews, and sauces usually are served with the starches. Unfortunately, sauces almost always contain meat, typically chicken (or lamb in the north). Grilled meat is popular in cities. Vegetables and fruit are fairly uncommon but can be found seasonally. Pesco-vegetarians will find that fish is available along the rivers. Bamako has a few European-style establishments that serve vegetable side dishes, pasta, and other welcome variations on the starch-sauce-meat theme.

French (p. 60) is the official language. **Bambara** is the most widely spoken indigenous language; in other West African countries, it is known as **Dioula**. Arabic (p. 112) is used in some regions. Hausa (p. 145) is spoken by some people in the eastern part of the country, and Pulaar (p. 143) is fairly common, especially in the north and west.

Bambara-Dioula

I would like something without _____.	Ne be _____tan doumounidofe.	nay bay _____ TAHN doo-moh-nee-DOH-fay
I do not eat _____.	Ne te _____ doun.	nay tay _____ doon

I eat _____.	Ne be _____lou du.	nay bay _____ LOO doo
meat	sogo	soh-goh
chicken	che	shay
fish	jege	jay-gay
eggs	chéfam	shay-FAHM
Thank you.	Iniche.	EE-nee-shay

Mauritania

Mauritania is not a very vegetarian-friendly destination. There are very few fruits or vegetables available outside of cities, although dates are fairly easy to find. The focus of most meals is meat such as lamb or camel, generally served with rice, millet couscous, or occasionally pasta. The northern part of the country is particularly bleak for vegetarians. There is somewhat more variety in the south, where some Senegalese influence creeps in. Nouakchott has several European restaurants serving pasta, pizza, or other such dainties. Pesco-vegetarians can find fish along the coast or in areas bordering the Senegal River.

The Hasaniya dialect of **Arabic** (p. 112) is the official language. French (p. 60), formerly the official language, is still widely used in business and government. **Wolof** (p. 149) is also an official language, and is spoken throughout much of the southern part of the country. Several other African languages are spoken, including **Pulaar** (p. 143), the language of a semi-nomadic people of the Sahel.

Pulaar

I would like something without _____.	Mido yidi ko alaa _____.	MEE-doh YEE-dee koh ah-LAH _____.

I do not eat ____.	Mi ñaamataa ____.	mee nyah-mah-tah ____
I eat ____ and ____.	Mido ñaama ____ e ____.	MEE-doh nyah-mah ____ ay ____
meat	teewu	tay-oo
chicken	ndiwri	ndee-wree
fish	liddi	lee-dee
eggs	boccoode	boh-choh-day
I am a vegetarian. *(literally, "I do not eat living things")*	Mi ñaamataa ko wadi fittaandu.	mee nyah-mah-tah koh wah-DEE FIH-tahn-doo
Thank you.	A jaaraama.	AH jahr-ah-mah

Niger

Restaurants in Niger tend to emphasize meat or fish on their menus. If you wish to avoid these items, you had better like millet, which is the main staple food throughout most of the country. Sorghum is also used. Millet is served with sauces that may or may not contain meat; spicy tomato sauce or peanut sauce is a common topping and is often meat-free. Millet and bean cakes with spicy powder and *meringa olifera* leaf balls with onion are common snacks. The daring may wish to try Niger's unique hard goat, sheep, or camel cheese (which may be highly unsanitary if uncooked). In the north, rice is the staple grain, and is usually served with lamb. Fish-eaters should gravitate towards the banks of the Niger River, where fish is served with particular frequency.

French (p. 60) is the official language. **Hausa** is spoken in the southern part of the country, while **Zarma** is spoken in the west. Pulaar (p. 143) is spoken by some of the nomadic tribes of the north.

Hausa

I would like something without ____.	Ina son wane abu wanda baya da ____.	EE-nah sohn WAH-nay AH-boo WAHN-dah BYE-ah dah ____
We would like something without ____.	Muna son wane abu wanda baya da ____.	MOO-nah sohn WAH-nay AH-boo WAHN-dah BYE-ah dah ____
I do not eat ____.	Ba ni chi ____.	bah nee chee ____.
but it is better to say (literally, "I am not used to")	Ban saba ba ____.	bahn SAH-bah bah ____
I eat ____ and ____.	Ina chi ____ da ____.	EE-nah chee ____ dah ____
meat	nama	NAH-mah
chicken	kaza	kah-ZAH
fish	kihi	kee-hee
eggs	kwe	kway
Thank you.	Na gode.	nah GOH-day

Zarma

I would like something without ___.	Ay ga ba hayfo kan sinda ___.	eye gah BAH hye-FOH kahn SEEN-dah ___
We would like something without ___.	Ir ga ba hayfo kan sinda ___.	eer gah BAH hye-FOH kahn SEEN-dah ___
I do not eat ___.	Ay si nwa ___.	eye seeg nah ___
I eat ___ and ___.	Ay ga nwa ___ da ___.	eye gah VAH ___ jah ___
meat	ham	hahm
chicken	gorno	GOHR-noh
fish	hamisa	hah-MEE-sah
eggs	gouri	goo-REE
Thank you.	Ay sa bo.	eye sah boo
or	Fofo.	foh-foh

Nigeria

Most Nigerians love meat but cannot afford to eat it on a regular basis. This means that restaurants almost always concentrate on meat—if someone is spending money on a meal out, they want flesh in their food. Similarly, as an honored guest in a home, it may be difficult to gracefully refuse to eat meat that has been prepared for you. Vegetarianism is not really understood in Nigeria, but it is sometimes accepted as one of those strange things foreigners do. Food stalls and takeaways are better bets for meatless dishes. The staple starches are pounded yam, cassava, and *gari* (fermented cassava meal); the starch is usually dipped in a soup or sauce based on peanuts, beans, or greens such as okra, spinach, or melon seed. Meat or fish is usually tossed in for people who can afford it. (Because foreign travelers invariably look like they can afford it, it is better to strike preemptively and ask that meat be left out.) Snack food such as bean cakes or french fries, although not especially healthy, are a good option because they usually contain no meat.

English is the official language, but there are over 400 indigenous languages spoken in Nigeria. The most common of these is **Yoruba**, which is spoken by more than a quarter of Nigerians, mainly in the southwest. **Ibo** is spoken in the southwest and in the Niger Delta area. Hausa (p. 145) is spoken by a large chunk of the population, mainly in the north and northwest.

Yoruba

I do not eat ____.	Iyi je ____.	ee-yee jeh ____
I eat ____.	Moman je ____.	moh-mahn jeh ____
meat	eran	eh-rahn
chicken	eran edire	eh-rahn eh-dee-ray
fish	eja	eh-jah
eggs	eyin	eh-yeen
Thank you.	Osehoun.	OH-shay-hoon

Ibo

	Ibo	
I do not eat _____.	A n'ahum eri _____.	ah NAH-hoom ay-ree _____
I eat _____ and _____.	A n'am eri _____ n' _____.	ah NAHM ay-ree _____ nah _____
meat	anu	AH-noo
chicken	anu okuko	AH-noo oh-kuh-koh
fish	azu	AAZ-oo
eggs	akwa	aak-WAH
Thank you.	Ndaewo.	nDAY-woh
or	Daalu.	DAH-loo

Senegal

Senegalese cuisine is often regarded as the best and most creative in West Africa. Unfortunately, Senegal is no more vegetarian-friendly than its neighbors. Rice or millet with sauce or soup is the basic pattern. As alluring as it may be in other respects, the sauce or soup usually contains meat or fish. Vegetables are often served as side dishes, but there are relatively few vegetarian main dishes. One exception is vegetable *mafé* served with rice and porridge. Rice and vegetables in tomato sauce can sometimes be found. Senegal's celebrated peanut sauce is typically made with chicken, although meatless versions can sometimes be found. Pesco-vegetarians should have no troubles in Senegal; the national dish is *tiebou djenn* (fish and vegetable stew), and fish in other forms is very common. In Dakar and other cities and large towns there are French restaurants and cafes and other European-style eateries that sometimes serve vegetarian entrees.

French (p. 60) is the official language. The most common African language, especially along the coast, is **Wolof**. Other languages such as Pulaar (p. 143), Mandinka (p. 139) and Bambara-Dioula (p. 142) are spoken in inland areas.

Wolof

I would like something without _____.	Dema büg lou amol _____.	DAY-mah buh-GUH loo ah-MOHL _____
I do not eat _____.	Duma lek _____.	doo-mah lehk _____
I eat _____ and _____.	Demai lek _____ ack _____.	deh-MYE lehk _____ ahk _____
meat	yap	yahp
chicken	ginar	GEE-nahr
fish	djenn	jyehn
eggs	nen	nehn
I am a vegetarian. *(Literally, "I do not eat living things.")*	Duma lek lui dunda.	doo-mah lehk loo-ee DOON-duh
Thank you.	Djer jeff.	jyehr jehf

149

Sierra Leone

When not engulfed in civil war, Sierra Leone has surprisingly decent food. As in the rest of the region, rice or tubers such as yams serve as the staple starch, and are served with sauce or soup. The soup is promisingly named by the main vegetable, but usually contains fish or meat. However, there is a small Lebanese population, and (often meatless) Middle Eastern food is sometimes available. There are also a few Indian restaurants in the larger towns. Snacks are often vegetarian; french fries are available in restaurants and food stalls, and are frequently made with white sweet potatoes. Steamed yams, fried plantains, and *fufu* (cassava balls) are all common.

Although **English** is the official language, Krio is the lingua franca. Since **Krio** is derived from English, the average English-speaker should be able to recognize plenty of phrases. Several tribal languages are also spoken.

Krio

I do not eat ____.	Ah no de et ____.	ah noh day eet ____
meat	mit	meet
chicken	fol	fahl
fish	fish	fish
eggs	eg	ehg
Please.	Ah beg.	ah behg
Thank you.	Thenki.	TEHN-kee

Togo

Togolese cuisine is much like the cuisine elsewhere in West

Africa: starches served with sauce are the rule. The good news is that the sauce in Togo tends to be somewhat more refined than in neighboring countries. Along the coast, most sauces contain fish; inland, many sauces are based on vegetables or greens, and meat costs extra. The starch component is likely to be rice or one of several *pâtes* (pasta-like substances) made from cassava, yams, or sometimes vegetables. Millet is common in the drier north. Grilled or fried plantain is a typical street food. Lomé has many European restaurants, and even a few Chinese and Middle Eastern restaurants.

French (p. 60) is the official language. The most common indigenous language is **Ewe**, which is spoken by close to half the population.

Ewe

I would like something without ____.	Medibe madu mu si me ____ me le o.	may-DEE-bay MAH-doo moo see meh ____ meh lay oh
I do not eat ____.	Nye me du na ____ o.	nyay meh doo nah ____ oh
I eat ____.	Me du na ____ o.	meh doo nah ____ oh
meat	lā	lah
chicken	koklolā	koh-kloh-lah
fish	akpavi	ahk-bah-vee
eggs	koklozi	koh-kloh-zee
Thank you.	Akpe	ahk-BAY

B. East Africa

East Africa is something of a culinary mixed bag for vegetarians. In some countries, such as Ethiopia and Eritrea, meatless dishes based on vegetables or legumes are quite easy to find. In other areas, almost everything is served with meat, at least in restaurants and at food stalls, although greens are sometimes available. Pesco-vegetarians should get by with few problems in most of East Africa, particularly near the sea or the Great Lakes. There is a substantial Indian population along the Indian Ocean littoral, and meatless dishes can usually be found at Indian-run restaurants.

Burundi

Burundi, riven by ethnic strife and poverty, does not have what one might call a world-class cuisine. Boiled starches such as corn, cassava, and plantain are the basics of the diet. The starches are usually accompanied by legumes, greens, stews (including peanut stew), and meat or fish. Fish is particularly common near Lake Tanganyika. Bananas and other fruit are relatively easy to find. There were formerly several excellent European restaurants in Bujumbura; very few remain, and those which survived are not particularly interested in vegetarian entrees.

French (p. 60) and **Kirundi** are the official languages. Swahili (p. 157) is spoken near the capital and in the eastern part of the country.

Kirundi

I do not eat ____.	Sindya ____.	SEEN-dyah ____
I eat ____.	Ndadya ____.	nDAH-dyah ____
meat	inyama	een-yah-mah
chicken	inkoko	ihn-HOH-koh
fish	ifi	ee-fee

eggs	amagi	ah-mah-gee
Thank you.	Urakoze.	oo-rah-KOH-zeh

Djibouti

The staple food of Djibouti is rice with fish or meat. It is also easy to find *lahooh* (a flat wheat bread similar to the *injera* of Ethiopia), which is often served with a sauce or soup made of vegetables or pulses, such as lentils. Spaghetti is reasonably common, although it is usually served with meat sauce. There are some Indian restaurants, and these may be the best options for vegetarian dishes. There is also a selection of French-style cafes and restaurants.

French (p. 60) and **Arabic** (p. 112) are both official languages. Somali (p. 160) is spoken by a large proportion of the population.

Ethiopia

Although few Ethiopians are actually vegetarians, there are plenty of meat-free dishes available around the country. (The relative abundance of vegetarian food is partly a result of the frequent meatless fasts undertaken by Ethiopian Orthodox Christians.) The base for most meals is *injera*, a spongy, unleavened bread made with wheat or sorghum. The *injera* is usually covered by or served with some sort of sauce or *wat* (stew). Typically, the sauce will contain meat or fish, but vegetable stew, lentil stew, and spiced vegetables are all common meatless alternatives. Greens and sometimes even cottage cheese are also occasionally available. In Addis Ababa and other large cities, there are some Western restaurants; pasta is a particular favorite at many of these establishments.

The official language of Ethiopia is **Amharic**. Tigrinya (p. 155) and several other indigenous languages are spoken in the provinces. Somali (p. 160) and Arabic (p. 112) are spoken in parts of northern Ethiopia. Italian and English are the most commonly-spoken European languages.

Amharic

Amharic is written in a lovely but difficult-to-reproduce script. The following phrases have been transliterated into the Roman alphabet.

I would like something without ____.	____ yelelebet mighib efelgalehu.	____ yeh-LEH-leh-beht mee-geeb eh-fehl-GAH-loo
We would like something without ____.	____ yelelebet mighib enfelegalen.	____ yeh-LEH-leh-beht mee-geeb ehn-feh-leh-gah-LEHN
I do not eat ____.	____ albelam.	____ ahl-beh-LAHM
I eat ____ and ____.	____ ena ____ ebelalehu.	____ EH-nah ____ eh-beh-lah-LEH-hoo
meat	siga	sih-gah
chicken	doro	doh-roh
fish	assa	ah-sah
eggs	inqulal	ihn-koo-LAHL
cheese	ayeb	eybh
Please.	Ebako.	eh-bah-KOH

Thank you.	Ameseghinalehu.	ah-meh-seh-GEH-nah-loo

Eritrea

Eritrea is a fairly easy country in which to be a vegetarian. Much of the population abstains from meat two days a week throughout the year, and for weeks at a time during Lent and the pre-Christmas period. Many grain and legume dishes (such as unleavened bread with spicy lentils) have been developed to deal with the meatless fasts; while these are obviously most easily available on fasting days, they can be found in some restaurants on any day of the week. Greens, assorted vegetables, and some kinds of fruit are all common, although the arid climate limits the range of fresh produce. As a result of Eritrea's long occupation by Italy, spaghetti and other kinds of pasta are popular, although they are often served with meat sauces.

Tigrinya is the main indigenous language, although several others are spoken. Because the country was a province of Ethiopia for decades, many Eritreans can speak Amharic (p. 154). Arabic is also useful. Some older people can speak Italian. Secondary education is now conducted in English, so the usefulness of English is likely to increase. English, Tigrinya, and Arabic are the main working languages of the government.

Tigrinya

Tigrinya uses its own writing system. The words and phrases below have been transliterated into the Roman alphabet.

I would like something without _____.	Zkone megbi bzey _____.	zuh-KOH-neh MEHG-bee bih-zay ____
I do not eat _____.	Ane ayblen ____ eyé.	ah-nay ay-beh-leh-ehn ____ EYE-eh

155

meat	sga	sih-gah
chicken	derho	dohr-hoh
fish	asa	ah-SAH
eggs	enquaquho	ehn-kwah-koo-hoh
I eat _____ and _____.	Ane _____ _____ yibele.	ah-nay _____ _____ yih-beh-LEH
meat	sgan	sih-gahn
chicken	derhon	dohr-hohn
fish	asan	ah-sahn
eggs	enquaquhon	ehn-kwah-koo-hohn
Please. *(female speaker)*	Bejaki.	beh-jah-KEE
Please. *(male speaker)*	Bejaka.	beh-jah-KAH
Thank you.	Yekenyeley.	yeh-kehn-YEH-lye

Kenya

The national dish of Kenya is *ugali* (cornmeal or millet porridge), potatoes, or rice served with stew. This combination can be found all over the country, but unfortunately the stew usually contains meat.

(Even vegetable stews are generally made with stock or gravy.) Vegetarians can sometimes supplement the starches with greens such as spinach, or occasionally with beans. Fortunately, fruit and fruit juice is widely available. Many Kenyans are of Indian descent and Indian restaurants, which almost always serve some vegetarian food, are found in cities throughout the country. These are especially common in Mombasa and elsewhere along the coast. Nairobi and Mombasa have quite a few Western-style restaurants that serve the usual suspects, including pasta. Most Kenyan game lodges offer their guests vegetarian entrees, although sometimes they must be requested in advance.

Although few people speak it as a native tongue except along the coast, **Swahili** is the *lingua franca* of Kenya and much of the rest of East Africa. Most Kenyans speak one of several tribal languages as their first language. **English** is also an official langauge, and is spoken by many Kenyans, especially in the cities.

Swahili

I would like something without ____.	Tafadhali ninitaka chakula bila ____.	tah-fah-DAH-lee nee-nee- TAH-kah chah-KOO-lah bee-lah ____
We would like something without ____.	Tafadhali tunaktaka chakula bila ____.	tah-fah-DAH-lee too-nahk-TAH-kah chah-KOO-lah bee-lah ____
I do not eat ____.	Sikuli ____.	see-koo-lee ____
I eat ____ and ____.	Kula ____ na ____.	koo-lah ____ nah ____
meat	nyama	nyah-mah

157

chicken	kuku	koo-koo
fish	samaki	sah-mah-kee
eggs	mayai	mah-yah-ee
Please.	Tafadhali.	tah-fah-DAH-lee
Thank you.	Asante.	ah-sahn-tay

Rwanda

Starches and legumes are the order of the day in Rwanda. Cassava or corn with beans and plantain or banana with split peas or beans is the typical meal. Rwandans who can afford it invariably add meat or fish, so most eateries do not concentrate on vegetarian basics. Some greens and vegetables can sometimes be found, and bananas are ubiquitous. Tea and coffee are the main crops, but you are unlikely to find them a satisfying option for long-term sustenance. There are very few Western restaurants left in the country, although more are likely to open in Kigali if peace can be maintained.

French (p. 60) is one official language; the other is **Kinyarwanda,** which is essentially the same language as **Kirundi** (p. 152). Swahili (p. 157) is also useful in many parts of the country.

Seychelles

The food of the Seychelles is a mixture of European, Indian, Chinese, and semi-indigenous Creole cuisine. Creole food is typically fish, pork, or chicken served with herbed rice. Vegetables such as calabash, eggplant, golden apple, red peppers, and choux choux are used in some dishes. Tropical fruit is reasonably common (as always, peel or wash very carefully in clean water) and fried or boiled bananas, sometimes made with coconut milk, are frequently served as a side dish. Starches such as cassava, sweet potato, and breadfruit are also common. There is a disturbing tendency to use fruit bat in stews and curries. Apart from the range of Creole cooking (which is not always easy to find in restaurants), there are Indian and Chinese restaurants on several islands and throughout Victoria; the former almost invariably serve vegetarian dishes. Hotel restaurants and other eateries catering to tourists tend to concentrate on European or "international" cuisine, with no particular emphasis on meatless food. Pasta is quite common, however.

French (p. 60) and **English** are the official languages, but French-derived Seychelles **Creole** is the first language of most islanders.

Creole

I do not eat _____.	Mon pa manz ____.	mawn pah mahnz ____
meat	la vyan	lah vee-ahn
chicken	le poul	luh pool
fish	le pwason	luh pwah-zahn
eggs	dizef	dee-zehff
Thank you.	Merci.	mehr-see

Somalia

Somalis have traditionally been nomadic herders, so milk and meat are important parts of the diet, and remain so today. (Constant factional warfare does not encourage settled agriculture.) Very few vegetables are consumed, although mangoes and bananas are grown locally, and vegetable curries can sometimes be found. *Injira*, Ethiopian-style unleavened bread, is a common food, but is usually covered with meat sauce. Rice and spaghetti (a legacy of Italian rule) are also frequently eaten, but again, they are typically served with meat sauce. Some towns have Indian or Middle Eastern eateries, which are the best choices for vegetarians.

Somali, a language derived from Arabic, is the national tongue. Swahili (p. 157) may be useful in the far south. Italian is potentially useful in the southern half of the country.

Somali

There are northern and southern dialects in Somali. The phrases and words below are in the northern dialect, but they should still be understood in other regions of the country. The phrases below have been transliterated into the Roman alphabet, from Somali Arabic script.

I would like something without _____.	Waxaan doonayaa cunto aan _____ lahayn.	wah-KHAHN doo-nah-YAH NN-toh ahn _____ lah-hyne
We would like something without _____.	Waxaan doonaynaa cunto aan _____ lahayn.	wah-KHAHN doo-nye-NAH NN-toh ahn _____ lah-hyne
I do not eat _____.	Ma aan cuno _____.	mah-ahn NN-oh _____
I eat _____ and _____.	Waxaan cunaa _____ iyo_____.	wah-KHAHN nn-AH _____ ee-yoh _____

meat	hilib	hih-lihbb
chicken	digaag	dih-GAHG
fish	kaluun	kah-LUHN
eggs	ukun	uh-kuhn
Please.	Walaal.	wah-LAHL
Thank you.	Mahadsamid.	mah-hahd-sah-meed

Sudan

Sudan is divided into two cultural and culinary worlds. The south of Sudan is culturally distinct from the rest of the country, and the food there (often in short supply, because of an ongoing civil war) is fairly typical of sub-Saharan Africa: millet, starches, stews, sauces, and greens are the norm. In northern Sudan, the food is much like that of Egypt and parts of the Middle East; *fuul* (kidney beans) with pita bread, lentil dishes, and soups and stews (sometimes vegetarian) are common dishes. Somewhat more variety is available in Khartoum, where there are a number of restaurants and cafes serving European or Middle Eastern cuisine.

Arabic (p. 112) is the official language and is spoken predominantly in the north. Indigenous African languages are spoken in the south of the country, and by refugees from the south. An aggressive policy of Arabicization is increasing the use of Arabic in southern regions.

Tanzania

Starches (especially corn) and beans are the mainstays of the Tanzanian diet. Stews are common accompaniments, but meat or fish is added whenever possible; fish is particularly common along the coast and near Lake Victoria and Lake Tanganyika. There are some meatless dishes based on peanuts, greens, pumpkin or other vegetables, or legumes such as chickpeas. However, these dishes are only incidentally meat-free: Tanzanians generally find the idea of vegetarianism to be incomprehensible or silly. Fresh fruit (peel or wash carefully) and coconuts are easily found. There is a small community of Indians along the coast so there are Indian restaurants (usually offering vegetarian dishes) in Dar es Salaam, Zanzibar, and elsewhere in the east. European food is served in hotels and game lodges, and in some restaurants in Dar, although vegetarian food is rarely a priority.

Swahili (p. 157) is the national language, although most Tanzanians speak something else as a native tongue. **English** is also an official language.

Uganda

Overall, Ugandan food is not particularly inspiring. Starch with meat is standard restaurant fare. However, all is not lost for vegetarians. There are some interesting meatless dishes such as *mugoyo* (sweet potato and white bean loaf), plaintains served with peanuts, and plain sweet potatoes and rice. There are also a few soups made with vegetables or greens, but these are not always easy to find outside Ugandan homes. Pesco-vegetarians will find plenty of fish near the lakes. There are a few Indian restaurants in the towns, and Kampala has a decent selection of Western food such as pasta.

English is the official language, and most Ugandans can speak it at least at a rudimentary level. A variety of tribal languages are spoken. Swahili (p. 157) can be very useful, especially in the eastern part of the country.

C. Central Africa

As elsewhere in Africa, starches with stews and sauces are the

162

basis of the Central African diet. Cassava is the cheapest and therefore most common starch, although rice, yam, or sometimes corn are also widely used. Stews and sauces usually contain meat or fish, although some are based solely on vegetables, greens, or peanuts. Much of Central Africa is tropical forest (although for how long is anyone's guess), and the denizens of the jungle—monkey, chimpanzee, crocodile, or even boa constrictor or elephant—are sometimes encountered on a plate. Because of deforestation, and probably also because people persist in eating them, these animals are becoming rarer and are not as commonly served as they once were.

Cameroon

Cameroon has some of the best food in Central Africa. The starches here include rice, millet "couscous" (nothing like the North African variety), and *pâtes* made from cassava, corn, plaintain, banana, and yam. The accompanying sauces are often delicious and complex, but frequently contain meat. Some tomato-based sauces are meatless, however. Okra, cassava leaf salads, or other vegetables and greens are often served as side dishes. Forest animals such as monkeys and more obscure creatures are often eagerly served up to foreigners in a mistaken belief that all tourists want to devour the local fauna. In Yaoundé and Douala there are some European-style cafes and other eateries that offer basic Western food.

Cameroon is a federation of former English and French colonies, so **English** and **French** (p. 60) are the official languages. However, English is not spoken much except in the western part of the country, while French is spoken in the rest of Cameroon. More than 20 major indigenous languages are spoken, including Pulaar (p. 143) and Hausa (p. 145). Arabic (p. 112) is spoken by some groups in the far north.

Central African Republic

The C.A.R. is quite poor, and the available food reflects this poverty. Apart from a few European restaurants in Bangui, most eateries serve meat or sometimes fish, with assorted starches and vegetable side dishes. Typical dishes include *gozo* (manioc paste), *ngunza* (manioc leaf salad), and assorted products of cassava. Greens-based soups such as spinach stew are fairly common, but sometimes contain chicken or other meat.

French (p. 60) is the official language, but the national language is **Sangho**. Arabic (p. 112) and Swahili (p. 157) are spoken in the far east of the country.

Sangho

I would like something without ____.	Mbi ye ti te mbeni ye ti sengue na ____ pepe.	mBEE yay tee tay mBAY-nee yay tee SAYN-gay nah ____ pay-pay
I do not eat ____.	Mbi te ye so ____ pepe.	mBEE tay yay soh ____ pay-pay
I eat ____ and ____.	Mbi te ____ si ____.	mBEE tay ____ see ____
meat	nyama	nyah-mah
chicken	kondo	kohn-doh
fish	soussou	soo-soo
eggs	parati kondo	pah-rah-tee kohn-doh
Thank you.	Singuila.	seen-GEE-lah

Chad

Chad is a poor, dry country with few natural resources or crops.

The diet largely consists of rice or millet with vegetables and meat; lamb is the most common meat in the north, while fish predominates in the region around Lake Chad. Peanuts are often added to vegetable dishes, especially squash and zucchini dishes. Okra is the standard vegetable accompaniment. Salads made from sweet potato leaves or other greens are also common, although not necessarily sanitary. There are a very few Western-style restaurants in N'Djamena, which cannot be counted on to offer vegetarian entrees.

French (p. 60) and **Arabic** (p. 112) are the official languages. Arabic is mainly used in the northern part of the country, while dozens of indigenous languages, including Sangho (p. 164), are spoken in the south.

Congo

Congolese cuisine is not very conducive to vegetarianism. Meat or fish is the centerpiece of most dishes, and it is difficult to find anything else. One could subsist on plain cassava or yam, although such a diet is neither healthy nor pleasant. Cassava leaves or other greens are sometimes available as side dishes. Bananas and papaya are fairly easy to get. There are some Europan restaurants and cafes in Brazzaville, but these generally concentrate on meat or fish dishes; a few restaurants serve pasta or other meatless entrees. Western-style restaurants may not serve vegetarian dishes as a matter of course, but are often willing to make meatless dishes if specifically requested to do so.

French (p. 60) is the official language. There are many indigenous African languages; the most common are **Kikongo** in southern Congo and Lingala (p. 167) in the north.

Kikongo

| I would like something without _____. | Mou zola kima ke'na _____ vé. | moo ZOH-lah KEE-mah kay-nah _____ vay |

I do not eat _____.	_____ mouké koudia vé.	_____ moo-kay KOO-dyah vay.
meat	ngombé	ngohm-bay
chicken	sousou	soo-soo
fish	mbisy	mbee-see
eggs	mêky	MAY-kee
Thank you.	Matondo mingi.	mah-TOHN-doh meen-gee

Congo, Democratic Republic (Zaïre)

Congo, formerly Zaïre, is a country that has been in the process of falling apart for the last quarter-century, so one should not expect a wide variety of tasty and creative vegetarian dishes. The typical meal is rice with sauce (often peanut sauce) and some kind of meat. Goat is the most common meat, but beef, chicken, and mystery animals from the jungle are also likely to turn up. Fish is eaten all along the substantial length of the country's rivers. Cassava and yams are sometimes cooked, mashed, and served like mashed potatoes. Most soups contain meat, but some are made with vegetables and greens. Nutritious but possibly unsanitary greens such as cassava leaves are fairly common. There are a few Indian and Lebanese restaurants in the cities, but far fewer than there once were. Kinshasa still has a few Western-style restaurants which may meet requests for meatless dishes.

French (p.60) is the official language, but hundreds of indigenous languages and dialects are spoken. The most useful may be **Lingala**, which was formerly the official language of the armed forces. Kikongo (p. 165) is spoken in western parts of the country; Kirundi (p. 152) and Swahili (p. 157) can be useful in the far east.

Lingala

I do not eat _____.	Ma koliya te _____.	mah koh-LEE-yah tay _____
I eat _____ and _____.	Ma liaki _____ ma _____.	mah lee-ah-kee _____ mah _____
meat	gombe	GOHM-bay
or	niama	nee-ah-mah
chicken	soso	soh-soh
fish	mbiusi	mBEE-see
eggs	maki	mah-kee
Thank you.	Malam.	mah-lahm

Equatorial Guinea

Equatorial Guinea is not particularly cosmopolitan in its cuisine. Rice, sweet potatoes and other tubers, and bananas form the basis of the diet; these are supplemented by fish on Bioko (the island portion of the country) and along the coastline and rivers of the mainland. Plenty of meat is eaten in inland areas, and animals such as antelope and monkey are likely to appear on your plate at some restaurants if you are incautious. Greens and vegetables are sometimes served as side dishes or toppings, and tropical fruit is easily to find.

Equatorial Guinea is unique among African countries in that **Spanish** (p. 70) is the official language. A pidgin English dialect is widely spoken. **Fang** is the predominant indigenous language on the mainland. The government has recently encouraged the use of French for better communication with Equatorial Guinea's Francophone neighbors.

Fang

I do not eat _____.	Ma jii _____.	mah jee _____
meat	chit	chihd
chicken	kub	koob
fish	cüas	kwahss
eggs	akii kub	ah-KEE koob
Thank you.	Akiba.	ah-KEE-bah

Gabon

Gabon is economically better off than many of its neighbors, and as a result meat is more frequently eaten here. Most Gabonese restaurants serve meat, including some meat from forest animals (although chicken and beef are more common). In food stalls and cheaper restaurants, starches such as yams and rice are served with spicy okra or other vegetables and greens; unfortunately, meat is usually added. In Libreville there are quite a few French cafes and restaurants which sometimes serve meatless dishes. Certain Western dishes such omelettes or french fries are common throughout the country.

French (p. 60) is the official language, and is widely used for inter-ethnic communication. Several different African languages are used in different regions of the country; Fang (p. 168) is the most common language in the northern part of the country.

São Tomé and Príncipe

This small, lush nation of two islands offers rather few culinary enticements to strict vegetarians. Fish, usually eaten with rice or occasionally tubers, is the mainstay of the diet. Some vegetables and greens are served, and tropical fruit is available, but otherwise there is little variety in the cuisine. Vegetarian soups or stews can occasionally be found.

Portuguese (p. 67) is the official language. While Portuguese is widely spoken as a second language, most people speak a Creole language called **Forro**.

Forro

I do not eat ____.	A mi na come ____.	ah mee nah koo-MAY ____
meat	cane	KAH-nee
chicken	ganha	gan-YAH
fish	peixe	pee-shee
eggs	ovo	AW-voo
Thank you. *(male speaker)*	Obrigado.	oh-bree-GAH-doh
Thank you. *(female speaker)*	Obrigada.	oh-bree-GAH-dah

D. Southern Africa

In general, southern Africa offers the greatest variety of food of any region on the continent (in part because it is generally better-off economically than other parts of Africa). Of course, there are significant exceptions to this generalization, and the food available, although varied, is not always vegetarian. Cornmeal is the main starch in this region, although rice or cassava are also used in some countries. In many southern African cities, African food is difficult to find, and Western-style food is prevalent. There are Indian restaurants in most cities in the region which reliably serve vegetarian dishes. Cheese is more common in southern Africa than in other parts of the continent.

Away from Portuguese-speaking Angola and Mozambique, and the island nations of the Indian Ocean, English is commonly spoken in southern Africa.

Angola

Land mines are scattered all over the country, an unwelcome legacy of Angola's long civil war. As a result, there is relatively little agricultural activity in the country, so food availability and variety are limited. Fish, especially cod, is the most popular meal near the coast, fresh water fish is consumed along the rivers, and beef and goat are consumed inland. Corn, rice, and cassava are basic starches and potatoes are also common in Angola, unlike in most African nations. Bananas and coconut are relatively easy to find. The few European restaurants in Luanda are largely closed, although some have reopened in the last few years. Restaurants in general tend to be very expensive.

Portuguese (p. 67) is the official language. A wide array of indigenous languages are in everyday use. Some Kikongo (p. 165) is spoken in the far north and in the Cabinda enclave.

Botswana

Landlocked and largely arid, Botswana is far from being a vegetarian's paradise. Meat is the focus of most meals, at least at restaurants and takeaways; game such as zebra and antelope is commonly purveyed to tourists. Maize porridge with beans is a standard Botswanan meal; this combination is typically served with meat or a cooked vegetable dish such as *morogo* (cooked spinach or other greens). Such food is not universally available at restaurants, however (especially at restaurants catering to travelers); steak and chicken with french fries is more usual fare. There are Indian restaurants in the towns, and these are the surest bets for vegetarian meals (although not even all Indian restaurants serve meatless dishes). Game lodges will often serve meat-free dishes, especially if an advance request has been made.

English is the official language. The primary language of everyday communication is **Setswana**, which is the native tongue of the vast majority of the population.

Setswana

I would like something without _____.	Ke batla sengwe kana _____.	kay baht-LAH sayn-gway gah-nah _____
I do not eat _____.	Ga ke je _____.	khah kay jee _____
I eat _____ and _____.	Ke ja _____ le _____.	kay jah _____ lee _____
meat	nama	nah-mah
chicken	koko	koo-koo
fish	tlhapi	taw-pee
eggs	mae	mah-ay
Thank you.	Ke itumetse.	kee too-MEHT-see

Comoros

Traditional Comorian cuisine is heavy on rice with fish or meat, and rather light on vegetarian dishes. Coconut is used in many Comorian dishes, and a few recipes call only for coconut and vegetables (but are difficult to find at restaurants). Some tropical fruit is available, just be sure to use the usual precautions and peel or wash carefully in clean water. Comoros is heavily touristed, and as a result there are many restaurants and hotels serving European-style food; some of these have vegetarian entrees such as pasta, but meatless dishes are generally not a high priority. There are a few Chinese and Indian restaurants lurking about.

French (p. 60) and **Arabic** (p. 112) are the official languages, although the use of French is generally disfavored. Most people speak Comorian, a blend of Swahili and Arabic, as a first language. Often, Comorians can understand basic Swahili (p. 157).

On **Mayotte**, a French overseas territory, there are many French-style cafes, bakeries, and restaurants, in addition to ordinary rice and seafood. French is spoken almost universally.

Lesotho

The standard meal in Lesotho, as in much of southern Africa, is *mielies* (cornmeal), often mixed with greens, and served with a stew made from meat, beans, peas, or vegetables such as eggplant or potato. French fries are a common snack, and in Maseru and other towns (Lesotho has no large cities), Western-style fast-food is the standard fare at most eateries. A few tourist-oriented lodges and hotels offer a more refined selection of food, including occasional vegetarian dishes.

SeSotho and **English** are the official languages.

SeSotho

As with many other southern African languages, SeSotho employs a number of different "click" sounds. Because they are difficult for the average English speaker to manage, the pronunciations below omit clicks. Although you will not be speaking proper SeSotho, you should still be understood.

I would like something without _____.	Ke batla ntho ntle _____.	kay baht-lah uhn-TOH uhn-tlay _____
I do not eat _____.	Ha ke je _____.	hah kay jee _____
I eat _____ and _____.	Ke je _____ le _____.	kay jee _____ lih _____
meat	nama	nah-mah
chicken	kgoho	khoh-hoh
fish	tchapi	kah-pee
eggs	mae	MAH-hee
Thank you.	Kea leboha.	kay-ah leh-BOH-ah

Madagascar

Most citizens of Madagascar are of Malay descent, and perhaps as a result, rice is the country's staple food. Except for that, Malagasy cuisine bears little resemblance to southeast Asian food. Cassava and corn are common starches. Spiced meat, fish, or vegetables accompany the starches and pure vegetarian dishes are rare in restaurants. Soups are popular, and greens are sometimes available. Tropical fruit remains abundant, although the country is losing forest cover and topsoil at such an alarming rate that soon it will be fortunate to have any trees left at all. Some

European food, especially French cuisine, is available in Antananarivo; there are also a few Chinese and Indian restaurants. **French** (p. 60) and **Malagasy** are the official languages.

Malagasy

I would like something without ____.	Mil zavatra tsy misy ____ izaho.	mee-lah ZAH-vah-trah tsee mees ____ ee-ZAH-hoo
I do not eat ____.	Tsy mihinana ____ izaho.	tsee mee-HEE-nah-nah ____ ee-ZAH-hoo
I eat ____ and ____.	Mihinana ____ sy ____ izaho.	mee-HEE-nah-nah ____ see ____ ee-ZAH-hoo
meat	hena	heh-nah
chicken	akoho	ah-koo
fish	trondro	trroon-drroo
eggs	atody	ah-TOO-dee
Please.	Azafady.	ah-zah-FAH-dee
Thank you.	Misaotra.	mee-SOW-trah

Malawi

Malawian food follows the general African model: Starch (here, usually corn or squash, or sometimes potato) is served with sauce or stew, which usually contains meat or fish. Some sauces are vegetarian; tomato sauce and peanut sauce are both common, and beans are sometimes used. Greens are frequently used in Malawian cooking; kale, pumpkin leaves, sweet potato leaves, and groundnut (peanut) leaves are all called into service. Along the shores of Lake Malawi, fish is the ubiquitous main dish and it is sometimes difficult to get anything else. Fruit, especially bananas, is easy to get. In Lilongwe and Blantyre there are many European-style restaurants, and even a few Indian and Chinese restaurants which, as always are often good places to look for meatless dishes.

English and **Chichewa** are the official languages. While most Malawians can speak one or both of these languages, several indigenous tongues besides Chichewa are in use around the country. A few people in the northeast can speak Swahili.

Chichewa

I would like something without _____.	Ndifuna kudya kuna _____.	ehn-dee-foo-nah kood-yah koo-nah _____
I do not eat _____.	Sindikudya _____.	seen-dee-kood-yah _____
I eat _____ and _____.	Ndikudya _____ na _____.	ehn-dee-kood-yah _____ nah _____
meat	nyama	nyah-mah
chicken	nkuku	ehn-koo-koo
fish	somba	sohm-bah
eggs	mazira	mah-zee-rah

Please.	Chonde.	chohn-day
Thank you.	Zikomo.	zee-koh-moh

Mauritius

As one expects of island nations, seafood is the main component of Mauritian cuisine. However, a polyglot of cultures co-exist here, and there are several options for vegetarians. Much of the population is of Indian descent, and Indian influences helped form the cuisine of Mauritius, so it is easy to get vegetarian food such as lentil dishes. For example, rice is the staple food, and although it is usually served with fish or fish sauce, it is generally accompanied by a range of vegetables or legumes. There are also many Indian restaurants serving traditional Indian fare, including vegetarian dishes. Chinese restaurants are also common. Although one hardly needs to resort to them, there are a number of restaurants serving European food, especially at hotels. (Italian food is particularly popular.) Fresh tropical fruit is available everywhere (peel or wash carefully).

English is (theoretically) the official language of Mauritius. French and Hindi are also used, but the vast majority of Mauritians speak a **Creole** dialect derived from French.

Mauritian Creole

I do not eat _____.	Mo pa mange _____.	moh pah mahnzh _____
meat	la viande	lah vee-AHND
chicken	poul	pool
fish	poisson	pwah-SAWN

eggs	disef	dih-zehf
Thank you.	Merci.	mayr-SEE

The nearby island of **Réunion** is a French overseas department. The range of produce is similar to that available in Mauritius, although there are more French-style restaurants and cafes and fewer Indian or Creole offerings. **French** (p. 60) is the official language.

Mozambique

Mozambican cuisine is somewhat more diverse than the food of many other poor African countries, and tends to be quite spicy. The basic food is beans with starch (usually rice) and meat or fish, but there are many variations on this theme. Unfortunately, most of these variations involve flesh of some kind. Seafood is king along Mozambique's lengthy coastline, while chicken is the main meat elsewhere. In restaurants, it may be difficult to get anything else, although there are some traditional vegetable side dishes such as *arroz de coco* (coconut rice) with tomatoes and chili. Since the countryside is still rife with landmines, fresh local vegetables are often in short supply. Plenty of coconuts and tropical fruits are available, however, and roasted cashews are a common street snack. In Maputo, there are a number of fancy European-style restaurants serving Portuguese, French, or Italian food; less upscale establishments serve pizza, french fries, croissants, and other potential vegetarian snacks.

Portuguese (p. 67) is the official language. Most Mozambicans can speak at least some Portuguese (although it may not be understood by everyone in remote areas). Hundreds of indigenous languages are spoken in Mozambique. Shona (p. 184) is spoken in parts of the northwestern provinces that border Zimbabwe. Some Swahili (p. 157) is used in the far north.

177

Namibia

As the wide variety of game dishes on menus attests, Namibia is not accustomed to catering to vegetarian travellers. Pesco-vegetarians will find that fish is usually available in restaurants, even away from the coast. Otherwise, in most parts of the country, cheese and tomato sandwiches and sad-looking salads are the order of day for anyone who wants to avoid meat. Because of Namibia's aridity, few vegetables are grown locally. Most Namibians ordinarily eat cornmeal porridge with beans and black-eyed peas, or sometimes cooked greens, but it is difficult to find such dishes outside Namibian homes. Somewhat more variety is available in Windhoek and Swakopmund; several restaurants in these cities are used to foreign travelers and offer meatless entrees.

English is now Namibia's sole official language. However, Namibia was occupied by South Africa for decades, and Afrikaans (p. 180) remains very useful. In addition, because Namibia was formerly a German colony, German is still used, especially in the coastal towns. Many indigenous African languages are spoken, particularly in northern Namibia.

South Africa

South Africa is a much more vegetarian-friendly place than it was just a few years ago (although the country is by no means problem-free). In the resort towns and in large cities, especially in Cape Town and the nearby winelands, an increasing number of restaurants offer palatable vegetarian entrees, and a few vegetarian-oriented restaurants and cafes have opened. Vegetarian meals are particularly easy to find in Durban, the center of South Africa's Indian community. In rural areas and small towns, however, it may be difficult to find a main dish that does not contain meat (particularly beef or lamb). Usually, basic sustenance such as toasted cheese-and-tomato sandwiches is the only viable option; vegans will be in dire straits indeed.

178

There is a tremendous difference between "white" or "Western" food and traditional African food. Most restaurants cater to a largely white clientele (who can usually afford to eat out more than the black majority), and serve familiar European-type foods. In many black South African eateries, however, the food is quite different: *pap* (cornmeal porridge, sometimes called bap) served with *samp* (a bean sauce) is the typical entree. Greens or vegetables are sometimes served on the side. Meat or chicken is included for anyone who can afford it (almost certainly including you). Although poverty limits meat consumption among much of the population, most Africans do not sympathize with intentional vegetarianism.

There are many ethnic eateries in the cities, offering everything from Mexican to Chinese to Indonesian to Middle Eastern cuisine; most such restaurants offer vegetarian entrees. Vegetarian travelers who wish to cook for themselves will find soy burgers, soy mince, tofu sausages, and the like at many supermarkets, although quality is often low. Fresh fruit and vegetables in South Africa are generally abundant and excellent.

Since the unlamented collapse of apartheid, the number of official languages has grown from two (English and Afrikaans) to eleven. **English** is spoken as a first or second (or third) language by a majority of the population. **Afrikaans** is the mother tongue of most white South Africans. It is also the first language of most mixed-race or "coloured" people in the western part of the country. If you must speak a European language to an African, English will often meet with a warmer reception than Afrikaans.

Xhosa is spoken by many Africans in the western part of the country and along the south coast. Zulu, which is similar to Xhosa, is spoken in the KwaZulu-Natal province in the southeast. SeSotho (p. 172) is spoken mainly in the central part of the country, and in some areas bordering Lesotho. Setswana (p. 171) is spoken in some areas in the north-central part of the country. All of these languages, and several more, are spoken in the townships around Johannesburg.

Afrikaans

I would like something without _____.	Ek will iets sonder _____ hê.	ehk vuhl ehts SOHN-duhr _____ hehr
We would like something without _____.	Ons will iets son-der _____ hê.	ohns vuhl ehts SOHN-duhr _____ hehr
I do not eat _____.	Ek eet geen _____ nie.	ehk eert khern _____ nee
I eat _____ and _____.	Ek eet _____ en _____.	ehk eert _____ ehn _____
meat	vleis	flayce
chicken	hoender	HEUN-duhr
fish	vis	fihs
eggs	eier	EYE-ehr
cheese	kaas	kahs
I am a vegetarian.	Ek is 'n vegetariër.	ehk ihss uhn veh-geh-TUH- rih-ehr
Please.	Asseblief.	uh-suh-BLEEF
Thank you.	Dankie.	DUHN-kee

Xhosa

Xhosa uses a range of different "click" sounds, which are difficult for English-speakers to manage. For ease of pronunciation, the clicks have been eliminated in the pronunciations given below. You will still be understood.

I would like something without _____.	Ndifuna nto enge-na _____.	n d e e - F O O - n a h nTOH ehn-geh-nah ____
I do not eat _____.	Andiyityi ____.	ahn-dee-yee-chee ____
I eat _____ and _____.	Nditya ____ nlay.	ndee-CHAH ____ nlay
meat	inyama	een-yah-mah
chicken	inkukhu	ihn-koo-koo
fish	intlanzi	ehnt-klahn-zee
eggs	amaqanda	ah-mah-KAHN-dah
Thank you.	Enkosi.	ehn-kohz

Zulu

Like Xhosa, Zulu uses a variety of clicks. For simplification, these clicks have been omitted from the pronunciations below.

I would like something without _____.	Ngicela ngiphe ____ ngaphandle.	ngee-keh-lah OO-ngee-peh ____ ngah-PAHN-dlay

We would like something without _____.	Sicela ngiphe _____ ngaphandle.	see-keh-lah OO-ngee-peh _____ ngah-PAHN-dlay
I do not eat _____.	Angiyidli _____.	ahn-GEE-yeed-lee _____
I eat _____ and _____.	Ngiyadla _____ ne _____.	NGEE-yah-dlah _____ _____ nay_____
meat	inyama	ihn-yah-mah
chicken	inkuku	ihn-koo-koo
fish	intlanzi	ihnt-LAHN-zee
eggs	amaqanda	ah-mah-kahn-dah
Thank you.	Ngiyabonga.	NEE-yah-bohn-gah
We thank you.	Siyabonga.	SEE-yah-bohn-gah

Swaziland

Swaziland is a small country with relatively little culinary variety. The typical Swazi meal is maize porridge and stew. Generally, eateries focus on meat or chicken dishes; vegetables are rare, although cooked greens are often eaten at home and are sometimes available in restaurants. Manzini and Mbabane have the standard assortment of European restaurants. There are Chinese restaurants in the towns where basic vegetable dishes are generally served; these are a better choice for meatless meals than many Swazi food outlets.

The official written language is **English**. In everyday conversation, most Swazis speak **siSwati**. SiSwati is essentially the same language as **Zulu** (p. 181).

Zambia

The staple in Zambia is *mielie* (cornmeal) porridge, which is eaten at virtually every meal. (Corn is also used to make Zambia's good beer.) The porridge is often accompanied by or mixed with greens such as spinach or pumpkin leaves. Sometimes the porridge is topped with stew, which might be made from peanuts, beans, tomatoes, or other vegetables. In most restaurants, meat or fish is included in virtually all dishes, including vegetable dishes; food stalls are more likely to offer meatless options (for cost reasons, not because of any vegetarian sensibilities). Cassava and sweet potatoes are also used as starches, especially in northern Zambia. In Lusaka and Livingstone, there are a few European and Indian restaurants that offer meatless entrees.

English is the official language. Many indigenous languages are spoken.

Zimbabwe

Zimbabwe's national dish is *sadza*, a maize porridge that is typically served with meat, beans, a peanut butter-based sauce, or greens such as spinach. Most small eateries serve *sadza*, but a variety of Western-style foods are also available throughout the country. Steak, for example, is quite popular (unfortunately for vegetarians) and french fries, potato chips, and assorted junk food can be found even in small towns. In Harare and Bulawayo, Indian, Chinese, Middle Eastern and other cuisines are available, and many of these restaurants serve vegetarian entrees. Most Zimbabwean game lodges and many hotels that cater to foreign tourists offer at least one (often utterly unimaginative) meatless option.

English is the official language, and most Zimbabweans can speak it. **Ndebele** and **Shona** are the most common languages in everyday use. Ndebele, which is spoken in the south and west, is very similar to **Zulu** (p. 181); the languages are mutually intelligible.

Shona

I would like something without ____.	Ndirikuta chunu chisina ____.	ndee-ree-KOO-tah choo-noo chee-see-nah ____
I do not eat ____.	Andigki ____.	ahn-dee-kee ____
I eat ____	Ndinodyka ____.	ndih-noh-chyuh-kuh ____
meat	nyama	nyah-mah
chicken	huku	hoo-koo
fish	hove	HOH-vay
eggs	mazai	muh-zah-ee
Please.	Ndapota.	ndah-POH-tah
Thank you.	Tatenda.	tah-TEHN-dah

chapter six
ASIA

sia is the largest continent and harbors a correspondingly vast array of cultures, cuisines, and languages. This
tremendous variety makes it difficult to generalize about the
availability of meatless food. In some Asian countries, such as
India, it is laughably easy to find vegetarian dishes; by contrast, it
is just about impossible to do so in parts of Central Asia. Most
often, however, it is of middling difficulty to obtain vegetarian
dishes—while they do not leap out at the traveler, they usually
can be found with reasonable effort. Strict vegetarians may have
problems in parts of southeast Asia, where fish sauce is a stealthy
and omnipresent ingredient even in many vegetable dishes. In the
(until recently) rapidly developing economies of some east Asian
countries, a greater variety of food is available; Western-style food
(including pasta and pizza) is growing increasingly popular.

There is no indigenous or European language that is particularly dominant on the continent, although certain languages are
widely spoken in their own regions. English is useful in former

British colonies, in tourist areas, and among many businesspeople in east Asia.

A. South Asia

It is a fairly easy task to find meatless dishes in most of south Asia. Hundreds of millions of vegetarian Hindus (and a few vegetarian Buddhists) live in this region, and their influence spills over even into non-Hindu areas. Dishes based on rice and pulses such as lentils are exceedingly common throughout the region, and are usually available even in Muslim-majority areas. In some cases, much more elaborate and interesting vegetarian dishes can be found which are definitely worth sampling (with caution—they are often very spicy). Cheese and yogurt are also fairly common in south Asia, although the cheese usually takes a soft, cottage cheese-like form. Western-style hard cheeses are relatively rare.

Because of the legacy of British colonialism, English is useful throughout most of south Asia, especially in the cities. In more remote areas, however, there may be few English speakers.

Bangladesh

Although there are few pure vegetarians in Bangladesh, it is virtually no problem to obtain vegetarian meals. Bangladeshis eat comparatively little red meat, although fish is extremely common (as befits a country that is largely under water for parts of the year). Obviously, fish-eaters will have an easy time in Bangladesh, but stricter vegetarians should never despair. Most restaurants have vegetarian dishes, while mung beans or rice and *daal* (lentils) are served at food stalls throughout the country. A variety of vegetables and interesting meatless snacks, such as *piaju* (an onion-lentil ball), are commonly available.

Bangla, or Bengali, is the national language. English is widely spoken as a second language.

Bangla

Bangla uses its own alphabet, which has been transliterated and modified in the phrases below.

I would like something without _____.	Ami _____ badey kichu khete chai.	ah-MEE _____ bah-DAY kee-choo kay-tay chye
We would like something without _____.	Amra _____ badey kichu khete chai.	ahm-RAH _____ bah-DAY kee-choo kay-tay chye
I do not eat _____.	Ami _____ khai na.	ah-MEE _____ kye nah
I eat _____ and _____.	Ami _____ ebong _____ khai.	ah-MEE _____ ay-bohng _____ kye
meat	mansho	mahn-shoo
chicken	murgi	MOOR-gee
fish	mas	muhss
eggs	dim	deem
cheese	ponir	poh-NEER
Thank you.	Dhonnobad.	DOH-noh-bahd

Bhutan

Assuming you can get into Bhutan (only a few thousand visitors per year are allowed in), you can bet that you will eat rice at almost every meal. The prevalence of rice is illustrated by the fact that the Bhutanese have no word for "food"; instead, the Dzongkha word for rice, *toh*, is used to mean food in general. Although the Bhutanese are quite fond of meat, there are a variety of dishes that are *jhaju* (prepared without meat). Many spicy vegetable dishes are meatless, and soft cheese is often used as a sauce on meat or vegetables. *Hemadatsi*, a chili and cheese paste served with rice, is a popular fast food item (the Bhutanese equivalent of pizza or hamburger in the United States). Potatoes, noodles, pancakes, and dumplings are all fairly common, although sometimes these are served with meat. In the south, lentils are the typical rice accompaniment.

Dzongkha is the official language. Dialects of Nepali (p. 198) and Tibetan (p. 216) are also spoken.

Dzongkha

The phrases below have been transliterated from Dzongkha script. See the Note on Tonal Languages (p. 6) in the Introduction for a description of the symbols used below. (Note however that tone is not as crucial in Dzongkha as it is in some other Asian languages such as Thai.)

I would like something without _____.	Gna toh _____ meba za we.	ngnah toh _____ may-bah sah wee
I do not eat _____.	Gna _____ me za.	ngnah _____ may sah
I eat _____ and _____.	Gna _____ da_____ za we.	ngnah _____ dah _____ sah wee
meat	sha	↘shah

chicken	jha sha	jah ⬎ shah
fish	gña sha	nyah ⬎ shah
eggs	gongido	gohng-ee-doh
cheese	da tshe	dah ⬏ tsee
Thank you.	Kadinche.	kah-deen-chay

India

India wins the award for the most vegetarian-friendly country in the world. It has over 800 million Hindus, none of whom eat beef, and many of whom are strict vegetarians. India has the additional distinction of hosting the world's only beef-free McDonald's (spiced vegetable patties and lamb-burgers make up the bulk of the menu). Certain standard meatless dishes, such as a combination of *daal* (lentils), rice, and *roti* bread, are available almost everywhere in India. In some areas, nothing else (meatless or otherwise) may be readily available, and a traveler might eventually get sick of eating these staples day after day. But Indian cuisine at its best is inventive and complex, and dishes and ingredients can vary significantly from region to region.

Southern India has the greatest concentration of strict vegetarians, so it has the greatest variety of vegetarian food which tends to be extremely spicy and is widely available as street food throughout India. Its most common forms are curries, pancakes or breads stuffed filled with spicy vegetables, and various creative incarnations of pulses served with rice. In northern India, somewhat more meat (usually lamb) is consumed, but there is still plenty of vegetarian food available, such as curried vegetables and dishes containing vegetables, cream or yogurt, and nuts. Cheese is a common ingredient in northern food; Indian cheese generally does not resemble typical

Western cheese, but is more like firm, small-curd cottage cheese.

The far north (Jammu and Kashmir) is home to the elaborate *wazwan* banquet, which usually features a number of meat dishes. Typically though, plenty of vegetable dishes are also featured.

The northwest is home to most of India's Muslims, and the region where the most meat is consumed. However, Muslims do not eat pork, and in India they tend not to consume beef. In Bengal, not much meat is consumed, although seafood is very common. A few of the Tibetans in Darjeeling are strict vegetarians, and some mock meat dishes are available there. If you desire a change of pace (although probably not from any lack of indigenous meatless options), Indian cities offer a variety of restaurants purveying the foods of Europe and North America, the Middle East, and east Asia. (Chinese food is particularly common).

India has an amazing number and variety of languages, many of which have over 1 million native speakers. **English** is an associate official language, and is spoken by most educated Indians. However, the primary official language is **Hindi**, which is spoken as a first language by almost a third of the population, mainly in the northern half of the country. Spoken Hindi is virtually identical to Urdu, which is spoken in the west of the country. Other important languages include **Gujarati**, spoken in the Gujarat state of western India; Bangla (p. 187), spoken in the Calcutta area; **Telegu**, used in Andhra Pradesh, in the southeast; **Marathi**, spoken in Maharashtra state in the west; **Tamil**, spoken in the far southern state of Tamil Nadu; Kashmiri (p. 200), spoken in Kashmir in the far north; Sindhi (p. 199), spoken in parts of western India; **Kannada**, used in Karnataka state in the southwest; and **Malayalam**, spoken in Kerala in the far southwest. Nepali (p. 198) is used in parts of northern India. Tibetan (p. 216) is spoken by the Tibetan exile community centered in Darjeeling.

NOTE: All of the indigenous languages of India use their own writing systems. The phrases and words listed below have been transliterated into the Roman alphabet.

Hindi

I do not eat _____. *(female speaker)*	Meñ _____ nahiñ khati.	mahn _____ nuh-heen kaht-TEE
I do not eat _____. *(male speaker)*	Meñ _____ nahiñ khata.	mahn _____ nuh-heen kaht-TAH
I eat _____. *(female speaker)*	Meñ _____ khati huñ.	mahn _____ kaht-TEE hoon
I eat _____. *(male speaker)*	Meñ _____ khata huñ.	mahn _____ kaht-TAH hoon
meat	gosht	gohshd
chicken	murghi	moorg-gee
fish	machhli	much-hlee
eggs	anda	uhn-dah
cheese	panir	puh-neer
I am a vegetarian.	Meñ shakahari huñ.	mahn shuh-kuh-huh-REE hoon
or		
	Meñ vegetarian huñ.	mahn vahg-gee-tay-ree-yuhn hoon
Thank you.	Shukria.	shoo-kree-yah

Gujarati

I do not eat_____. *(male speaker)*	Huñ _____ khato nathi.	hoon _____ KAH-toh nah- TEE
I do not eat____. *(female speaker)*	Huñ _____ khati nathi.	hoon _____ KAH-tee nah-TEE
I eat_____ and_____.	Huñ _____ ane _____ khaoun chhu.	hoon _____ ah-nay _____ kown choo
meat	maas	mahns
chicken	kookda	koh-koh-dah
fish	machhli	mahch-hlee
eggs	inda	ihn-dah
I am a vegetarian.	Huñ sakahari chhu.	hoon shah-KUH-huhrr-ee choo
Please.	Maherbani.	mayr-bah-nee
Thank you.	Abhaar	AHB-hahr

Telegu

I do not eat _____.	Nenu _____ thinanu.	nay-NOO _____ tee-nah-noo
I eat _____.	Nenu _____ thin-taanu.	nay-NOO _____ teen-TAH-noo

meat	maamsamu	mahm-sah-moo
chicken	kodi	koh-dee
fish	chepalu	chay-pah-loo
eggs	gudlu	good-loo
I am a vegetarian.	Nenu saakhahaari.	nay-NOO sah-kah-hah-REE
Thank you.	Meeku naa krithagnathalu.	mee-koo nah kree-tuhg-nah-tah-LOO

Marathi

I do not eat _____.	Mi _____ khaat naahi.	mee _____ kaht nah-HEE
I eat _____ and _____. *(female speaker)*	Mi _____ aani _____ khaate.	mee _____ ah-nee _____ kah-TAY
I eat _____ and _____. *(male speaker)*	Mi _____ aani _____ khato.	mee _____ ah-nee _____ kah-TOH
meat	maañs	mahns
chicken	kombadi	KOOM-bah-dee
fish	maasa	mah-sah

193

eggs	andi	uhn-DEE
I am a vegetarian.	Mi shaakaahaari aahe.	mee shah-kah-hah-REE ah-HAY
Please.	Krupaya.	KROO-pye-yah
Thank you.	Dhanyawaad.	DAHN-yuh-wahd

Tamil

I do not eat _____.	Naan _____ sapida matten.	nahn _____ sah-PEH-dah mah-TAYN
I eat _____.	Naan _____ sapiduven.	nahn _____ saw-peuh-doo-VAYN
meat	mamisam	mahm-sahm
chicken	kozhi	koh-lee
fish	meen	meen
eggs	muttai	moo-tye
I am a vegetarian.	Naan sutha saivam.	nahn soo-tah sye-hvahm
Thank you.	Nanri.	NAHN-drree

Kannada

I do not eat _____.	Nanu ____ thin-nuvudhilla.	nah-NOO ____ teen-noo-voo-dehl-LAH
I eat _____.	Nanu ____ thin-nuthene.	nah-NOO ____ teen-noo-tay-nay
meat	maamsa	mahm-suh
chicken	koli	koh-lee
fish	meenu	mee-noo
eggs	motte	moht-tay
I am a vegetarian.	Nanu sasyahari.	nah-NOO sahs-yah-hah-ree
Thank you.	Dhanyavadagalu.	dahn-yah-vah-dah-gah-loo

Malayalam

I do not eat _____.	Njan ____ thin-nathilla.	n-jahn ____ teen-nah-teel-LAH
I eat _____.	Njan ____ thin-narundu.	n-jahn ____ teen-nah-roon-doo
meat	irachi	ee-rah-chee
chicken	kozhi	koh-lee

fish	meenu	mee-noo
eggs	mutta	moo-tuh
I am a vegetarian.	Njan oru sasya-bhukkanu.	n-jahn oh-roo sahs-yahb-boo-kah-noo
Thank you.	Nanni.	nah-nee

Maldives

Although the epitome of a beautiful tropical archipelago, the Maldives have poor soil and very few fruits or vegetables are produced locally. (Coconuts and breadfruit are the main exceptions.) The staple meal is rice and curry; sometimes the curry is meatless, although fish is the most common ingredient. Apart from this typical fare, there are relatively few options. A few Chinese restaurants exist, as well as some Indian restaurants that usually serve South Indian vegetarian food. The hotel restaurants serve Western food; Italian food is a particular favorite.

The national language is **Divehi**. Government officials can usually speak English.

Divehi

Divehi uses its own script, derived from Arabic and Sinhalese writing. The phrases below have been transliterated into the Roman alphabet.

I do not eat _____.	Aharen nukan _____.	ah-HAH-rehn noo-KUHNN _____

I eat ____ and ____.	Aharen kan ____ adhi ____.	ah-HAH-rehn kuhnn ____ ahd-dee ____
meat	egkamo mas	ehg-KAH-moh mahs
chicken	kukulu	koo-koo-LOO
fish	kandu mas	kahn-DOO mahs
eggs	bis	beese
Thank you.	Sukuria.	soo-koo-REE-ah

Nepal

It is generally very easy to get meatless dishes in Nepal. The typical meal in Nepal is rice with *daal* (lentils) and vegetable curry. This will probably be the most common meal for most travelers, vegetarian or not. Other vegetable dishes, such as potatoes or carrots, are also widely available. Although Nepalis are generally not as consciously vegetarian as many of their Indian neighbors, it is highly unlikely that meat will ever be imposed on you. In Kathmandu, a variety of cuisines is available, including Chinese, Indian, and Western. There are also a number of restaurants catering predominantly to European, Australian, and North American travelers; almost all of these establishments serve meatless dishes, and some specialize in vegetarian food.

Nepali is the official language. Other languages such as Tibetan (p. 216) and assorted Indic and Central Asian-derived tongues are also spoken.

Nepali

Nepali has its own script. The phrases below have been transliterated into the Roman alphabet.

I do not eat _____.	Ma ____ khandina.	muh ____ kahn-DEE-nuh
I eat _____ and _____.	Ma ____ ra ____ khanchhu.	muh ____ rruh ____ kunch-HOO
meat	maasu	MAH-soo
chicken	kukhura	koo-koo-rah
fish	maachhaa	MAHCH-hah
eggs	phul	fool
cheese	chij	cheedz
I am a vegetarian.	Ma saakaahaari huñ.	muh sah-kah-hah-ree hoon
Thank you.	Dhanyabhad.	DAHN-yahb-bahd

Pakistan

Unlike their Hindu neighbors in India, most Pakistanis (the vast majority of whom are Muslim) eat substantial amounts of meat. Nonetheless, vegetarian options are available with a minimum of fuss. South Asian standards such as rice and *daal* (lentils), roti bread, and curried vegetables can be found throughout most of the country. Southern Pakistan has quite a few interesting vegetable side dishes, containing pumpkin, potato, spinach or other greens. These, however, become somewhat more scarce the further north you go. In the cities, a fairly wide variety of food is available, including Chinese, Middle Eastern, and Western food.

English and **Urdu** are both official languages. In spoken form, Urdu is virtually the same as Hindi (p. 191); the written forms differ, however. Other major languages include **Sindhi**, spoken in the southeast; **Kashmiri**, spoken in the far northeast; and Pashtu (p. 203), spoken in the north. NOTE: All the languages listed below use non-Roman distinct writing systems. The phrases and words have been transliterated into the Roman alphabet.

Sindhi

I do not eat _____.	Aauun _____ na khaaiindo aahiyaañ.	ah-oon _____ nah kyne-doh ah-hee-yahn
I eat _____.	Aauun _____ khaaiindo aahiyaañ.	ah-oon _____ kyne-doh ah-hee-yahn
meat	gosht'u	gohsht-oo
chicken	kukkarr'u	kook-kuhrr-oo
fish	machii'u	muh-chee-oo
eggs	baida	byde-duh
cheese	paneer'u	puh-neer-oo
Thank you.	Meherbaanii.	meh-hehr-bah-nee

Kashmiri

I do not eat _____. (*male speaker*)	Ba'h chhus ni _____ kheyvaan.	buh ch-hoos nih _____ kay-vahn
I do not eat _____. (*female speaker*)	Ba'h chhes ni _____ kheyvaan.	buh ch-hehs nih _____ kay-vahn
I eat _____.	Ba'h chhus _____ kheyvaan.	buh ch-hoos _____ kay-vahn
meat	syun	syoon
chicken	kokkur	kohk-koor
fish	gaad	gahd
eggs	thul	tool
cheese	kra'r	kruhr
Thank you.	Shukria.	shoo-kree-uh

Sri Lanka

Almost without exception, the main meal in Sri Lanka is curry with rice. As befits an island nation, fish is often eaten with or in addition to these basics; meat is also sometimes used. Fortunately, the curry used is frequently a vegetable curry, as there are plenty of Sri Lankan vegetarians (although only a minority of the population is Hindu, mainly in the north). Lentils are also commonly eaten (usually in addition to the obligatory rice and curry). There are many varieties of stuffed breads, which can be delicious. In Colombo, and to a lesser extent in other Sri Lankan cities, Chinese and Western restaurants abound in case your palate needs a break from fiery spices.

Sinhalese is the official language. Tamil (p. 194) is spoken in the north of the island. English is widely spoken as a second language.

Sinhalese

Sinhalese uses its own writing system; the Sinhalese script has been transliterated into the Roman alphabet below.

I do not eat _____.	Mama _____ kanne nae.	mah-muh _____ kuh-NAY neh
I eat _____ and _____.	Mama _____ saha _____ kanawa.	mah-muh _____ suh-huh _____ kuh-nuh-vuh
meat	mas	muhss
chicken	kukulmas	koo-kool-muhss
fish	malu	mah-loo
eggs	bittara	bee-tuh-RUH
Please.	Karunakara.	kah-roo-NAH-kah-ruh
Thank you.	Bohoma sthuthi.	boh-HOH-muh STOOT-tee

B. Central Asia

In the case of the six Stans (which is not the name of a Hardy Boys mystery but rather the six countries of Central Asia:

Afghanistan, Kazakhstan, Tajikistan; Uzbekistan, Turkmenistan, and Kyrgyzstan) vegetarians must take care not to be overly particular. This part of the world is the home of hard-fighting, hard-riding, and hard-living people who are unlikely to be sympathetic to vegetarian sensibilities about eating animals. In fact, meat, along with fermented milk, forms the core of the diet in much of the region. Since these countries are overwhelmingly Muslim, avoiding pork usually will not be a concern. In very remote areas with a tradition of aggressive hospitality, it might be best to give up vegetarianism temporarily (some travelers have actually been threatened by nomads when they refused to share their meat). Otherwise, it is possible to live (although not happily) on starches. In some areas, during the summer and fall, there is excellent produce such as apricots, grapes, and apples.

Thanks to past Soviet domination and occupation, Russian (p. 99) is commonly spoken as a second language throughout Central Asia. Very little English is spoken. Most of the languages in this region use the Cyrillic alphabet, but are theoretically in the process of Romanizing their writing systems. Therefore, the words and phrases below have been presented (perhaps over-optimistically) in the Roman alphabet.

Afghanistan

While here, as elsewhere in Central Asia, lamb and other meats form the core of the diet, Afghanistan is probably the most vegetarian-friendly (or more accurately, least vegetarian-hostile) country in the region. Traditional Afghan cuisine includes a number of vegetable dishes containing, for example, eggplant, pumpkin, or potatoes. Lentil and split pea dishes are fairly common, although these may be cooked in meat stock. Almost everything is served with unleavened bread or rice; sometimes the rice gets gussied up into more substantial forms. Other options may include vegetable soup (but beware of meat stock), *boulani* (turnovers, usually filled with vegetables), or Afghan noodles.

Kabul formerly offered a comspomolitan array of cuisines but nearly two decades of war have understandably changed things dramatically.

Dari, a dialect of Persian, is spoken by over half the population. **Pashtu** is spoken by another third. Other Persian dialects and Central Asian languages, including Uzbek (p. 210) and Turkmen (p. 209), are spoken by the remainder of the population. Both Dari and Pashtu use their own writing systems, which have been transliterated into the Roman alphabet below.

Dari

I do not eat _____.	Man nemeekho-ram ____.	mahn neh-meekh-oh-rahm ____
I eat _____ and _____.	Man ____ wo ____ meekhoram.	mahn ____ woh ____ meekh-oh-rahm
meat	goosht	goosht
chicken	morgh	mohrk
fish	mahi	mah-HEE
eggs	tokhme-morgh	tohkh-meh-mohrk
cheese	panir	pah-NEER
Please.	Lotfan.	loht-FAHN
Thank you.	Mamnun.	mahm-NOON

Pashtu

I do not eat _____.	Za'h ____ na kho-ram.	zah ____ nah khohd-rahm

203

meat	wokha	woh**kh**-hah
chicken	chargha	chahr-gah
fish	mahi	mah-hee
eggs	eggae	eh-gay
I am a vegetarian.	Za'h yu zabzikore yem.	zah yoo zuhb-zee-kohr yehm

Kazakhstan

In Kazakhstan, it is virtually anathema not to eat meat. Indeed, the consumption of meat is something of a ritual, and some Kazakhs may take offense—or at least think you foolish and rude —if you do not partake. Since Kazakhstan has a large Russian Orthodox minority, meatless dishes should, in theory at least, be available during traditional fasting periods. However, the reality is that they can usually only be found in private homes. Cheese, yogurt, and other products made from sheep's milk are common. There are plenty of starches, mainly rice and potatoes, to provide carbohydrates. In the summer, a variety of fruits, vegetables, and nuts can be bought in markets, although restaurants do not always take advantage of this bounty. Apples are available in the autumn. Finally, pesco-vegetarians will find plenty of dried fish (this fish is intentionally dried for consumption as opposed to the dead, dry fish left behind by the rapidly receding Aral Sea).

Kazakh is the official language, but is spoken as a mother tongue by less than half the population. The main language of commerce and inter-ethnic communication is Russian (p. 99), which is spoken as a first or second language by over two-thirds of the population. Other Central Asian and Slavic languages are also spoken.

Kazakh

I would like something without ____.	____ tamak bolsa jeymin.	____ tah-mahk bohl-sah zhay-meen
meat	etsiz	eht-SEEZ
chicken	tawïqsïz	tah-weuk-SEUZ
fish	balïqsïz	bah-leuk-SEUZ
eggs	jumïrtqasïz	zhuh-meurt-kah-SEUZ
cheese	sïrsïz	seur-SEUZ
or	kurïtsiz	koo-reut-SEEZ
I do not eat ____.	Men ____ jemeymin.	mehn ____ zhay-may-meen
I eat ____ and ____.	Men ____ jäne ____ jeymin.	mehn ____ zhuh-neh ____ zhay-meen
meat	et	eht
chicken	tawïq	tah-WEUK
fish	balïq	bah-LEUK
eggs	jumïrtqa	zhoo-meurt-KUH
cheese	sïr	seur
or	qurït	koo-REUT
Thank you.	Raxmet.	rahkh-meht

Kyrgyzstan

Kyrgyzstan is paradise for confirmed carnivores and more like hell for vegetarians. The diet is centered around meat, especially lamb and mutton. The meat is usually accompanied by fermented sheep, goat, or camel milk, and yogurt is sometimes available. The milk is also made into cheese, and imported Russian cheese is also available. Obviously, vegans are in for an especially nasty time. Vegetables are few and far between at restaurants, although they can be found at markets in the summer. Rice and other starches are also available. Vegetarians who want any variety or nutrition in their diet would be wise to bring cooking equipment and supplies.

Kirghiz is the official language, and is the mother tongue of slightly more than half the population. Russian (p. 99) is widely used. A small minority speaks Uzbek (p. 210).

Kirghiz

I would like something without _____.	_____ tamak bolso jeymin.	_____ tah-mahk bohl-soh dzhay-meen
meat	etsiz	eht-SEEZ
chicken	tooksuz	toh-ohk-SOOZ
fish	balïksiz	bah-leuk-SEEZ
eggs	jumurtkasïz	dzhoo-moort-kah-SEUZ
cheese	sïrsiz	seur-SEEZ
or	kurutsuz	koo-root-SOOZ
I do not eat _____.	_____ jebeym	_____ dzheh-baym

I eat _____ and _____.	_____ jana _____ jeym.	_____ dzhah-nah _____ dzhaym
meat	et	eht
chicken	took	toh-ohk
fish	balïk	bah-LEUK
eggs	jumurtka	dzhoo-moort-KAH
cheese	sïr	seur
or	kurut	koo-ROOT
Thank you.	ïrakmat.	EU-rahk-maht

Tajikistan

As elsewhere in Central Asia, meat forms a large part of the Tajik diet. However, Tajik cooking has been modifed by Persian, Indian, and Chinese influences, so the range of choices is somewhat wider than in other former Soviet republics. Vegetable dishes are relatively common, although meat is sometimes added. Curries, *nan* (unleavened bread), rice and lentils, and other Indian-type food is sometimes available. Rice is the most widely used starch, and it is sometimes made into pilafs or other more complex dishes; these often contain meat or are made with meat stock, however. Outdoor markets are a good source for fresh vegetables and fruit in summer, (just remember to peel or wash carefully in clean water). **Tajik**, a Persian dialect, is the official language. Russian (p. 99) is still widely spoken as a second language. About a quarter of the population speaks Uzbek (p. 210).

Tajik

I do not eat _____.	_____ nämixoräm.	_____ nuh-meekh-oh-ruhm.
I eat _____ and _____.	_____ wo _____ mixoräm.	_____ woh _____ meekh-oh-ruhm
meat	gušt	goosht
chicken	morgh	mohrk
fish	mahi	mah-hee
eggs	toxmä	tohkh-mah
cheese	panir	pah-neer
Please.	Lotfen.	loht-FEHN
Thank you.	Motşäkäram.	moht-shuh-kuh-ruhm

Turkmenistan

Vegetarians in Turkmenistan deserve hardship pay, because the Turkmen diet consists almost exclusively of meat and milk products. Commonly consumed meats include camel, horse, lamb, and mountain goat. This fleshy diet is supplemented by the fermented milk of sheep, goats, and camels, and sometimes bread or rice. It is certainly possible to subsist on these supplements although such a diet may not be to everyone's liking. (Vegans, of course, will be especially deprived.) A few soups or more elaborate rice dishes make their appearance from time to time, although these are likely to contain meat or at least meat stock. Fish are eaten along the Caspian Sea, so pesco-vegetarians can find some relief there.

Turkmen is the national language. Almost everyone can speak Russian (p. 99) as a first or second language. There is also a minority population of Uzbek (p. 210) speakers.

Turkmen

I would like something without ____.	_____ nahar bolsa īyerin.	____ nah-hahr bohl-sah eye-yeh-REEN
meat	etsiz	eht-SEEZ
chicken	tovuksïz	toh-vook-SEUZ
fish	balïksïz	bah-leuk-SEUZ
eggs	yumurtğasïz	yoo-moort-gah-SEUZ
cheese	sïrsïz	seur-SEUZ
or	päynirsiz	pay-neer-SEEZ
I do not eat ____.	_____īymerin.	____ eye-meh-reen
I eat ____ and ____.	_____ve_____īyerin.	____ veh ____ eye-yeh-reen
meat	et	eht
chicken	tovuk	toh-VOOK
fish	balïk	bah-LEUK

eggs	yumurtğa	yoo-moort-gah
cheese	sir	seer
or	päynir	pay-NEER
Thank you.	Täşäkkür.	tuh-shuhk-KOOR

Uzbekistan

While Uzbeks are as fond as meat as any self-respecting Central Asian people, vegetarians will find Uzbekistan to be relatively manageable, especially in the summer. For a start, over 1000 varieties of melons are grown here. A fitting variety of other fruits and vegetables are also cultivated, and in Uzbekistan these are often incorporated into common dishes. Pumpkin, squash, eggplant, and spinach are all typical ingredients, and plain steamed vegetables are sometimes available as a side dish. (Obviously, variety is substantially lessened during the winter months.) Legumes such as lentils and mung beans are often served with rice. Rice pilaf is common, but is usually cooked in meat stock. A common snack is *samsa* (small pies, usually with meat fillings, but occasionally filled with vegetables). Unleavened *nan* bread is a standard accompaniment to most meals.

Uzbek is the principal language. Russian (p. 99) is spoken as a first language by a small ethnic Russian minority, and as a second language by much of the population.

Uzbek

I would like something without ____.	____aş bolsa yermän.	____ ahsh bohl-sah yehr-MUHN
meat	estiz	eht-SEEZ

chicken	tavuksiz	tah-vook-SEEZ
fish	baliksiz	bah-leek-SEEZ
eggs	tuxumsiz	tookh-oom-SEEZ
cheese	sïrsiz	seer-SEEZ
or		
	kurutsiz	koo-root-SEEZ
I do not eat ____.	____yemäsmän.	____ yeh-muhs-muhn
I eat ____ and ____.	____vä____ yermän.	____ vuh ____ yehr-muhn
meat	et	eht
chicken	tavuk	tah-VOOK
fish	balik	bah-LEEK
eggs	tuxum	tookh-OOM
cheese	sïr	seer
or		
	kurut	koo-ROOT
Thank you.	Raxmat.	rahkh-maht
or		
	Täşäkkür.	tuh-shuhk-koor

C. Northeast Asia

On the whole, while the countries of northeast Asia do not present insurmountable hurdles to visiting vegetarians, vegetarianism as such is not widely practiced despite substantial Buddhist influence. Nonetheless, meat traditionally has not figured as the centerpiece of most cuisines in this region (with the exception of Mongolia). In addition, many northeast Asians will eat occasional vegetarian meals for health or spiritual reasons, so a request for a meatless meal is not particularly bizarre in itself. Life is particularly easy for pesco-vegetarians in most areas, because fish is often an integral part of the diet. Rice is available almost everywhere but, while it can always serve as vegetarian insurance, it can also become tiresome.

Dairy products are not normally consumed in this part of the world, and items like cheese are usually only found in Western restaurants or in some supermarkets. ("Cheese eater" is sometimes used in China as a perjorative term for a Westerner.) Vegans should not necessarily rejoice, because eggs are very commonly eaten in northeast Asia.

China (People's Republic)

As one would expect in such a vast country, traditional Chinese cooking varies from one region to another, from the carbohydrate-heavy foods of the north to the notoriously spicy food of Sichuan in the south. Unfortunately for vegetarians, most of the regional cuisines work most of their magic with dishes that include at least some meat. It is certainly possible to get vegetarian food in China, but vegetarians will tend to miss out on the subtleties of regional variation. (This may be a good thing: do you really care to relish the different techniques used to cook chicken feet?)

That said, many Chinese take short vacations from meat consumption for reasons of health and balance. (The idea of permanent, intentional vegetarianism remains poorly understood, however.) To facilitate this practice, some vegetarian restaurants have sprung up, and although they are not ubiquitous, they can be found in most cities. Chinese vegetarian cooks are esteemed for the degree to which vegetarian food can be made to resemble meat, so you should not necessarily be alarmed if you are served a so-called vegetarian dish that looks like it has chunks of chicken in it. Even away from specialty vegetarian restaurants, it should not be a Herculean task to obtain meatless food. Stir-fried vegetables or bean curd (tofu) dishes are fairly easy to find. Of course, rice is served with most meals. Noodles are also very common, but they are sometimes served in meat broth.

A somewhat greater range of offerings is available in the larger cities. **Hong Kong** has the greatest variety of restaurants by far: vegetarian restaurants, Indian restaurants, European restaurants, American fast-food chains, restaurants serving dishes from all the regions of China and elsewhere in east Asia are all thick on the ground. Whether such bounty will continue to be available in the next few years of Chinese rule remains to be seen. Other Chinese cities are far less cosmopolitan. Beijing and Shanghai have a decent selection of Asian and Western restaurants, and Western-style food can be found in most of the eastern cities, at least in hotels, but the range is limited.

In mainly Buddhist Tibet, vegetarianism is not exactly common, but it is generally respected. Common vegetarian dishes include vegetarian dumplings, meatless noodle soup, and fake meat (for the monks). Barley dishes, grain porridges, vegetable potstickers (*sei mo-mo*) and stir-fried or steamed vegetables are also common.

Dairy products are uncommon in China, although yogurt and fermented milk can be found in western China.

Chinese is not a single language, but is divided into different dialects. **Mandarin** (also called *Putonghua*, or common language) is the official language, and most Chinese can speak it, at least as a second language. There are many additional—and mutually incomprehensible—dialects spoken around the country. The most prominent is **Cantonese**, which is spoken in Guangdong province and in Hong Kong. Assorted other non-Chinese languages are spoken by minority groups; these include Korean (p. 222), **Tibetan** in Tibet (although the Chinese government has been trying for years to eliminate its use), and **Uygur**, spoken by Central Asian Muslims in the far west and northwest of the country. Outside of Hong Kong, relatively little English is spoken except by university students and workers in the tourist industry.

All Chinese languages employ their own writing systems, which have been transliterated in the phrases below. (Uygur is often Romanized, however.) See the Note on Tonal Languages (p. 6) in the Introduction for a description of the symbols used below.

Mandarin

I would like something without ____.	Wo xiang chi dianr bu dai ____ de.	chee wǒh sheěahng deeanzh ➚ boo ➘ dye ____ deu
I do not eat ____.	Wo bu chi ____.	chee wǒh ➘ boo ____
I eat ____ and ____.	Wo chi ____ he ____.	chee wǒh ____ ➚ heu ____
meat	rou	➘ roh
chicken	ji	jee
fish	yu	➚ eu

214

Asia

eggs	dan	↘dahn
I am a vegetarian.	Wo chi su.	wǒh ᶜʰᵉᵉ ↘ soo
Thank you.	Xiexie.	↘sheah-sheah

Cantonese

I do not eat ____.	Ngo hmm sic ____.	↘umm sihk ____ ➚ngoh
I eat ____ and ____.	Ngo sic ____.	sihk ____ ➚ngoh
meat	yuk	yohk
chicken	gai	gye
fish	yui	➚jooee
eggs	dan	dahn
I am a vegetarian.	Ngo sig tsai.	dzeye ➚ngoh sihk
Thank you. *(for making a simple request or buying something)*	Hmm goi.	goy ↘umm

215

| Thank you. (when receiving a gift or special favor) | Doh tse. | doh dzeh |

Tibetan

In Tibetan, tones are not nearly as important as they are in Chinese or Cantonese. If you fail to use them, you will still be understood; you will merely sound peculiar. All English speakers know at least one Tibetan word: *yak* means yak.

I do not eat ____.	Nga ____ sa gi mei.	ngah ____ suh gee may
I eat ____.	Nga ____ sa gi yö.	ngah ____ suh gee yeu
meat	sha	shuh
chicken	cha	chuh
fish	nya	nyuh
eggs	go nga	goh ngah
Thank you.	Tü ji che.	too jee cheh

Uygur

| I do not eat ____. | ____ yemäsmän. | ____ yeh-muhs-muhn |
| I eat ____ and ____. | ____ vä ____ yermän. | ____ vuh ____ yehr-MUHN |

216

meat	et	eht
chicken	toxu	toh-**KHOO**
fish	beliq	beh-**LEEK**
eggs	tuxum	too-**KHOOM**
cheese	kurut	koo-**ROOT**
Thank you.	Räxmät.	rahkh-maht

Macau, a Portuguese colony that is due to become a special administrative region of the People's Republic in 1999, has many Portuguese and other Western restaurants (as well as restaurants serving southern Chinese-style cuisine). Although Cantonese is the main language of the people, **Portuguese** (p. 67) is the official language. (Mandarin will probably replace Portuguese after the handover.)

Japan

The price of beef in Japan might drive the most ardent carnivore to vegetarianism. However, there is surprisingly little intentional vegetarianism among the Japanese. Pesco-vegetarians will find Japan to be almost heaven (and those who eat *fugu* fish, deadly if not properly prepared, could literally go there). Those who avoid flesh entirely will have a harder time, but should be able to eat reasonably well. Cooked vegetables, such as boiled spinach, are available as side dishes in most restaurants. Heartier sustenance is provided by the amazing variety of Japanese noodles. The two main varieties are *udon* noodles, made from wheat flour, and *soba* noodles, made from buckwheat flour; however, they are usually dipped in sauce or served in broth that is not necessarily vegetarian. Rice is of course ubiquitous, and is typically served plain, although this may not be the most satisfying meal. Another common food is *tempura*, vegetables or seafood dipped in batter and deep-fried in vegetable oil. There are many varieties of vegetable or soy soups (but chicken broth is often added). Some *sushi* is vegetarian—made of raw vegetables rather than raw fish.

World cuisines are well-represented in Japanese cities. Restaurants serving other Asian cuisines are particularly common. These often feature meatless dishes. Italian restaurants and other Western-style restaurants are found in urban areas, although they tend to be very expensive.

Most restaurants in Japan have window displays of plastic or wax replicas of the dishes they serve. While the presentation may not be the most appetizing, and it is not always easy to distinguish vegetarian from non-vegetarian dishes, the displays make life slightly easier for befuddled or culture-shocked travelers.

Japanese is the national tongue. Many Japanese learn English in school, but they are not always proficient at speaking it.

Japanese

Japanese uses a complex set of characters; the phrases below have been converted to the Roman alphabet.

I would like something without _____.	_____ no haittenai shina o kudasai.	_____ noh HYE-tay-nye shee-NAH oh KOO-dah-sye
I do not eat _____.	Watashi-wa _____ o tabemasen.	WAH-tah-shee wah _____ oh tah-bay-mah-sehn

I eat _____ and _____.	Watashi-wa _____ to _____tabemas.	WAH-tah-shee wah _____ toh _____ tah-bay-mahss
meat	niku	NEE-koo
chicken	toriniku	TOH-dee-nee-koo
fish	sakana	sah-kah-nah
eggs	tamago	TAH-mah-goh
cheese	chizu	CHEE-zoo
I am a vegetarian.	Watashi-wa saishoku-shugisa desu.	WAH-tah-shee wah SYE-shoh-koo shoo-GEE-sah dehss
Please. (used only if asking for a special favor; not to be used casually)	Onegaishimasu.	oh-nay-gye-shee-mahss
Thank you.	Arigatou gozaimasu.	ah-dee-gah-toh goh-zye-ee-mahss

Mongolia

The word "variety" would never be used to describe the diet of a vegetarian (or non-vegetarian for that matter) in Mongolia. The country is almost entirely rural, and many Mongolians still live nomadic, pastoral lives. Most Mongolians make due on mutton combined with various bland starches (especially potatoes), cabbage, yogurt and hard cheese; a vegetarian will have to subsist on a standard Mongolian diet, minus the mutton. Because the country has no seacoast and is quite arid, fish does not figure prominently in Mongolian cuisine except near lakes. Ulan Bator is marginally more cosmopolitan than the rest of the country, and some Western, Russian, and Chinese food is available. However, even in the capital, the smell of mutton hangs heavily in the air. As Mongolia ends its Soviet-imposed isolation, more culinary choices presumably will become available to the traveler.

Mongolian (Khalka Mongol), a Turkic language, is the national tongue. Russian (p. 99) is a common second language, especially among older people. A few other Turkic languages are spoken.

Mongolian

Traditional Mongolian script is beautiful and ornate; however, its use has been discouraged over the last 50 years in favor of Cyrillic. However, the traditional script is once again becoming popular, and the Roman alphabet is also more commonly seen. The words and phrases below are the Romanized versions of Mongolian script.

I do not eat _____.	Bi _____ iddeggûi.	bih _____ ihd-deh-KWEE
I eat _____ and _____.	Bi _____ iddeg.	bih _____ ihd-dehk
meat	max	mah**kh**
chicken	taxia	tah**kh**-ee-ah
fish	zagas	zah**kh**-ahss
eggs	ōndog	ohn-duhk

220

| cheese | byaslag | BEE-ah-slahk |
| Thank you. | Bayarlalaa. | bye-ahr-lah-LAH |

North Korea

While North Korea may be a mystery wrapped inside an enigma, the food is no surprise: rice, when it is available, is the staple of the North Korean diet. In those rare times when there is enough for all to eat, North Korean food is similar to that of its counterpart south of the DMZ. When harvests are poor (as they often are), vegetarians are unlikely to have any problem avoiding meat: North Korean television has been known to broadcast tips on "tasty ways to prepare grass". It is best for travelers to avoid North Korea altogether at such times.

Korean (p. 222) is the national language.

South Korea

Traditionally, meat has not been the focus of Korean cuisine. Unfortunately, it has become very common in the last quarter-century but it is usually not served in huge quantities. In Korea, rice is the centerpiece of the meal, so it is always possible (although boring and not particularly healthy) to eat plain rice. Rice in its various permutations is served with side dishes, which are sometimes meatless, but more frequently do contain meat. The most famous vegetable dish is probably the notorious, fermented vegetable concoction *kimchi*, which is pickled and often spicy (a few varieties may contain fish). Other possible side dishes include seasoned vegetables, or tofu or vegetable stews and soups. (Be careful though, many of the soups contain meat or fish or are made with meat stock.) Noodles made from wheat, buckwheat, or potato are fairly common, but watch out for meat or meat broth.

It can be difficult to find any substantial vegetarian options at many restaurants, as main courses are almost uniformly meaty, and even vegetable side dishes may contain meat or fish. (Pesco-vegetarians should survive well in most places, however.) Some back-alley restaurants pose further dangers by serving esoteric foods such as dog or earthworm soup. If it proves positively impossible to find a vegetarian option at a Korean restaurant (or if rice with vegetables becomes tiresome), other cuisines can easily be found in the cities. Chinese, Japanese, and all manner of Western food is commonly available.

The national language is **Korean**.

Korean

Korean uses its own alphabetical system, which has been transliterated into the Roman alphabet below.

I would like something without ____.	Nanŭn ____ an dŭrŏhgan gŏsul mŏkgo shipsŭm-nida.	nah-neun ____ ahn teu-loh-gahn keu-seul muh-koh shihp-seum-nee-dah
We would like something without ____.	Wurinŭn ____ an dŭrŏhgan gŏsul mŏkgo shipsŭm-nida.	woo-ree neun ____ ahn teu-loh-gahn keu-seul muh-koh shihp-seum-nee-dah
meat	kogi-ga	koh-kee-kah
chicken	takgogi-ga	tah-koh-gee-kah
fish	saengsŏn-i	sahng-suhn-ee

222

eggs	kyeran-i	geh-rahn-ee
I do not eat ____.	Nanŭn ____ an mŏksŭmnida.	nah-neun ____ ahn muhk-seum-nee-dah
I eat ____.	Nanŭn ____ mŏksŭmnida.	nah-neun ____ muhk-seum-nee-dah
meat	kogi-rŭl	koh-kee-leul
chicken	takgogi-rŭl	tah-koh-gee-leul
fish	saengsŏn-ŭl	sahng-suhn-eul
eggs	kyeran-ul	geh-rahn-eul
I am a vegetarian. (*This phrase implies that the speaker eats no animal products whatsoever.*)	Nanŭn chaesik chuŭija imnida.	nah-neun cheh-sihk joo-oy-chah ihm-nee-dah
Thank you.	Kamsahamnida.	kahm-sah-hahm-nee-dah

Taiwan

Taiwanese food does not vary dramatically from the food consumed across the Taiwan Straits in the People's Republic. While meat and fish are very common, items such as stir-fried vegetables, noodles, and bean curd are also easily available. Many Taiwanese occasionally abstain from meat, and most cities and even some smaller towns have vegetarian restaurants. Generally, mock meat made from soya is served at these establishments, although more vegetable-oriented dishes are also available. Many ordinary restaurants will also serve meatless dishes upon request. Rice is, of course, available everywhere and served with everything.

Taiwan is somewhat more Westernized than the People's Republic, and it is possible to find Western-style fast food, and sometimes more formal establishments serving European or American dishes. Taipei and Kaohsiung are good places to seek variety. Other Asian cusines are represented, especially in the cities.

Mandarin Chinese (p. 214) is the official language, and virtually everyone on the island can speak it as a first or second language. Many people speak other Chinese dialects, especially Taiwanese or Hakka, as a first language.

D. Southeast Asia

In theory, southeast Asia should be easy pickings for vegetarians: fresh vegetables are common ingredients, tropical fruit is bountiful, and vegetable oil is usually used for cooking. In practice, however, southeast Asian cuisine poses hidden culinary perils. Chicken, pork, and beef are well-loved (as are many animals less familiar to Westerners), but are easy enough to spot and avoid. The real problem arises with the way seafood is used, particularly in fish sauce. In many parts of the region, fish sauce is added liberally to all sorts of dishes, and it is often difficult to determine which food contains fish sauce and which does not. (Obviously, this will not be a problem for pesco-vegetarians.)

There are a few vegetarian restaurants scattered around the region's main cities. In areas frequented by Western travelers, many restaurants offer meatless dishes. Chinese restaurants, which generally have at least one vegetarian option, can be found in most large towns. Rice is the staple food throughout southeast Asia, so it will always be possible to get your fill of this ubiquitous starch. As in other east Asian countries, cheese is not a common food.

Brunei

This tiny but rich country has rather few dining options, much less fantastic offerings for vegetarians. Rice and meat are the staples but if you happen to be able to eat petroleum (Brunei's main export) then you might enjoy dining here. There are a few Indian and Chinese restaurants, which are probably the only viable options for meatless entrees. There are also a few Western-style restaurants, mainly in hotels, which sometimes offer vegetarian dishes.

The official language is **Malay,** which is identical in all important respects to Bahasa Indonesia (p. 227). English is a common second language.

Cambodia

Although there are vegetarian restaurants in Phnom Penh, Siem Reab, and a few other towns, Cambodia is not a particularly vegetarian-friendly place. Western-style food such as pizza is available in the cities. Apart from these urban amenities, vegetarian pickings are slim. As in every other country in southeast Asia, rice, usually served with meat, is the staple food. It is usually possible to order main dishes without meat, but the concept of vegetarianism is difficult for most Cambodians to understand, and some people may try to slip broth or bits of meat into food to keep vegetarians from growing "too weak." With luck, despite your "weakened" state, you may stumble across indigenous vegetable dishes, such as *cha tra kouen* (fried water lily, usually served with bean paste). It is quite possible to provide for yourself (albeit leanly) here: French-style baguettes are available in most towns, all manner of luscious fruit can be found, and there are plenty of meatless snacks such as *trakoowen* (morning glories) and *sandayk dai* (peanuts). Pesco-vegetarians will have a much easier time, because fish is commonly eaten in most parts of the country.

Khmer is the official language. French is still widely used as a hangover from colonial days.

Khmer

Khmer uses its own alphabetical script, which has been roughly transliterated into the Roman alphabet below. Unlike other southeast Asian languages, Khmer is not tonal.

I would like something without _____.	Kyoum choal chit moap oait mian _____.	k-nyohm chohl cheht m-hohp OTT mee-uhn _____
I do not eat _____.	Kyoum niam _____ mun ban te.	k-nyohm nyahm _____ meun bahn tay
I eat _____.	Kyoum niam _____.	k-nyohm nyahm _____
meat	sait	syte
chicken	sait mourn	syte moh-ahn
fish	trey	truh-ee
eggs	poang mourn	poh-ahng moh-ahn
Thank you.	Ar goun.	ahr koon

Indonesia

The exact range of food available in Indonesia varies from

island to island. Generally, it should not be too difficult to find vegetarian dishes. While chicken and fish are standard everywhere, and obscure forest animals are frequently eaten on Borneo, they are by no means the only options available. Rice is the staple food throughout the country, but Indonesian cuisine employs lots of other grains, legumes, tubers such as cassava, and vegetables, cooked in a variety of ways (coconut milk is a particularly common ingredient). Tofu and tempeh are also widely used. One of the most well-known Indonesian dishes is *gado gado*, steamed vegetables or greens with peanut sauce; it is usually perfectly acceptable for vegetarians. The rice table is another good option: a wide selection of dishes is placed before you, many of which will probably be meatless, and you (usually) pay only for what you eat. However, in some areas of the country, fish sauce is added to many dishes and it is not immediately obvious which dishes contain this ingredient.

Most Indonesian restaurants will prepare meatless dishes on request, even if nothing suitable appears on the menu. In the cities, Western food is easily available, and meatless dishes are often available there. In areas frequented by tourists, some specialty vegetarian restaurants exist, and most ordinary restaurants will serve at least a few vegetarian dishes. Bali has a particularly wide selection of vegetarian-friendly restaurants.

Dozens of languages are spoken in Indonesia. To ease inter-group communication, **Bahasa Indonesia** (often just called Bahasa) was adopted as the national tongue; it is spoken by virtually everyone in the country as a first or second language. **Javanese**, which (as one would expect) is spoken on Java, has the most native speakers of any Indonesian language.

Bahasa Indonesia

I would like something without ____.	Saya mahu makanan tanpa ____.	suh-yuh muh-oo muh-kuh-nuhn tuhn-puh ____

We would like something without _____.	Kami mahu makanan tanpa _____.	kah-mee muh-oo muh-kuh-nuhn tuhn-puh _____
I do not eat _____.	Saya tidak makan _____.	suh-yuh tee-duhk muh-kuhn _____
I eat _____ and _____.	Saya makan _____ dan _____.	suh-yuh muh-kuhn _____ duhn _____
meat	daging	duh-gihng
chicken	daging ayam	duh-gihng eye-yuhm
fish	ikan	ee-KUHN
eggs	telur	tuh-LOORR
cheese	keju	kay-joo
Thank you.	Terima kasih.	teh-REE-muh KAH-see

Javanese

Javanese has several complex levels of formality that vary depending on the relationship between speaker and addressee. In order to avoid offense, the phrases used here are somewhat formal. Although you can safely use them, you may sound unnaturally stiff and distant in some contexts.

| I do not eat _____. | Kula mboten nedha _____. | koo-luh boh-tehn nehd-hoh _____ |

I eat _____ and _____.	Kula nedha _____ lan _____.	koo-luh nehd-hoh _____ luhn _____
meat	daging	duh-gihng
chicken	pipik	pee-pee
fish	iwak	ee-wuh
eggs	endog	uhn-DOHK
Thank you.	Matur nuwun.	MAH-toor noo-woon

Laos

Most Laotians are accustomed to eating all types of meat. As one would expect, vegetarianism is neither widely practiced nor well-understood; even Buddhist monks eat meat. Pesco-vegetarians should have no problems, because fish is an extremely common food, especially in towns along waterways. Stricter vegetarians might ask for a vegetable dish such as stir-fry, but it is likely to contain oyster sauce or *nam paa* (fish sauce). Fish sauce is added to almost every recipe, although if you ask nicely people may try to accommodate you and leave the fish sauce out. Since rice is served with everything, plain rice is always an option. Sweetened sticky rice is also common.

Lao is the official language. Lao is broken up into many different dialects, some of which are closer to Thai (p. 236) than to standard Lao. There are also several minority ethnic groups with their own languages. Many older people speak French.

Lao

Lao has its own writing system, which has been transliterated into the Roman alphabet below. Lao is a highly tonal language; see the Note on Tonal Languages (p. 6) in the Introduction for a description of the symbols used below.

I do not eat ____.	Khoy gin ____ bo dai.	↘koy geen ____ boh ↘dye
I eat ____.	Khoy gin ____ dai.	↘koy geen ____ ↘dye
meat	sin	↘sheen
chicken	sin gai	↘sheen gye
fish	paa	pah
fish sauce	nam paa	↘nuhm pah
eggs	khai	kye
Thank you.	Khawp jai.	↘kawp jye

Malaysia

Traditional Malay cooking is not particularly oriented towards vegetarianism. Nonetheless, it is not difficult to eat well and avoid meat here. The major cities have specialty vegetarian restaurants, usually run by ethnic Chinese (who make up about a third of the population). These serve Chinese-style vegetarian food, such as mock meat and fish, or tofu and vegetables. There is also a significant Indian minority in Malaysia, so Indian restaurants are very common and almost always serve vegetarian dishes. Food stalls usually serve some meatless dishes, such as rice and mixed vegetables. A more elaborate and fairly common offering is veg-etarian banana leaf rice—rice served on a banana leaf with 3 different vegetable dishes. The cities and resort areas have plenty of Western-type food; pizza and pasta are particularly popular. Those who prefer to picnic will find a magnificent selection of tropical fruit. Soy milk is readily available.

Malay is the main national language. It is identical in virtually all respects to Bahasa Indonesia (p. 227). English is widely spoken in most parts of the country, especially in major cities and resort areas. A large proportion of the population is of Chinese descent; these people still speak dialects of Chinese. Many ethnic Indians speak languages such as Tamil (p. 194) and Hindi (p. 191). Tribal languages are spoken in Malaysian Borneo.

Myanmar (Burma)

Burmese cuisine is an interesting amalgam of Indian, Thai, and Chinese cooking styles. As in neighboring countries, the staple food is rice, often made into a variety of interesting dishes, such as the ubiquitous, rich and rather cloying *mon't lone yay baw* (floating rice balls). The rice is accompanied by meat or vegetable dishes; obviously, the latter are more interesting to vegetarians. Stir-fried vegetables or greens such as watercress are quite common; unfortunately, they are often served with fish sauce. Vegetable curries are also easily available, including unusual varieties such as pumpkin curry, gourd curry, or bean curry. Again, however, fish sauce is sometimes added. Vegetable soups are common. For example, gourd soup is served in many restaurants and virtually every food stall. But, while the soup may be free of fish sauce, it typically is made with shrimp powder. There are some interesting meatless snacks, such as gourd strips with bananas in garlic and vinegar sauce, split pea fritters, onion fritters, and steamed eggplant.

Besides traditional Burmese cuisine, Indian and Chinese restaurants are very common, and are good sources of meatless dishes. Indian dishes generally do not contain fish sauce. In Rangoon and Mandalay, Western food is popular, and such tasty treats as pizza and pasta are available.

231

Burmese is the national language. There are also several different ethnic groups which use their own languages.

Burmese

Burmese uses its own writing system; the words and phrases below have been transliterated into the Roman alphabet. Burmese is also tonal; see the Note on Tonal Languages (p. 6) in the Introduction for a description of the symbols used below.

I would like something without ____.	____ ma ba beh sa ba meh.	sahr ____ muh pahr beh	bah meh
I do not eat ____. *(male speaker)*	Cha-naw ____ ma sa bu.	NAW chuh ____ muh	sahr boo
I do not eat ____. *(female speaker)*	Cha-ma ____ ma sa bu.	MUH chuh ____ muh	sahr boo
I eat ____. *(male speaker)*	Cha-naw ____ sa ba de.	NAW chuh ____	sahr bah deh
I eat ____. *(female speaker)*	Cha-ma ____ sa ba de.	MUH chuh ____	sahr bah deh
meat	aa thaa	ah THAH	
chicken	che' tha	cheht thah	
fish	nga	ngah	
eggs	oo	↘oh	

232

		cheh soo
Thank you.	Che-zu tin ba de.	tihn nah deh

Philippines
The Philippines presents two faces to vegetarians. On one hand, vegetarianism is growing in popularity, particularly in urban areas. Most cities now have one or more specialty vegetarian restaurants, and many upscale non-vegetarian restaurants offer meatless entrees. At the same time, most Filipinos, particularly in rural areas, do not have a firm grasp of the concept of vegetarianism. For example, when ordering a "vegetarian" pizza, you might be asked what meat you would like as a topping. Rice remains the staple food throughout the country, and despite the growing but still small number of vegetarians, it is usually accompanied by fish or pork. In some areas, *aso* (dog) is eaten, although the government is discouraging its consumption (especially in front of tourists). Vegetables (with rice) make a decent meal, but they are often served with meat or with the stealth ingredient *patis* (fish sauce). In towns, if no vegetarian restaurant is available, Chinese restaurants can usually be found, and Western-style food is always popular and may sometimes provide a meatless alternative (non-vegetarian "vegetarian" pizzas notwithstanding).

Tagalog is the national language. English is an official language and is commonly spoken, while dozens of local languages are used in the provinces.

Tagalog

I would like something without _____.	Gusto ko po sana ng walang _____.	GOO-stoh koh poh sah-nah **ng** wah-lah**ng** _____

We would like something without ____.	Gusto namin po sana ng walang ____.	GOO-stoh nah-meen poh sah-nah **ng** wah-lahng ____
I do not eat ____.	Hindi ako kumakain nang ____.	heen-dee ah-koh koo-mah-kah-een nahng ____
I eat ____ and ____.	Kumakain ako nang ____ at ____.	koo-mah-kah-een ah-koh nahng ____ aht ____
meat	karne	KAHR-nay
chicken	manok	mah-NOHK
fish	isda	ees-DAH
eggs	itlog	eet-LOHG
cheese	keso	KAY-soh
Please.	Paki.	pah-kee
Thank you.	Salamat.	sah-LAH-maht
Thank you. *(Respectful, said to elders)*	Salamat po.	sah-LAH-maht poh

Singapore

Singapore is a cosmopolitan and compact city-state with a

refreshingly wide variety of food packed into a small area. The Chinese are the dominant ethnic group in Singapore, and many of China's regional cuisines are represented here. Chinese-style vegetarian food is available in almost all food courts and hawker stalls, and there are several specialty vegetarian restaurants. These often make mock meat dishes (such as the seemingly oxymoronic vegetarian sweet and sour pork). There are many traditional Malay food outlets, but most specialize in poultry dishes; some vegetable side dishes are usually available, however. Plenty of Indian restaurants can be found in Singapore, and as one would expect, these often serve wonderful vegetarian meals (banana leaves are sometimes used in place of plates). Other Asian and Western cuisines are also widely available.

Singapore has four official languages: Chinese (**Mandarin**) (p. 214), **Malay** (p. 227), **Tamil** (p. 194), and **English**. Generally, English works well, as most Singaporeans can speak at least some English as a second language. The other languages are used by their respective ethnic groups (Chinese, Malay, and Indian).

Thailand

Despite a long Buddhist tradition, and contrary to the impression that Thai restaurants create in the West, very little Thai food is purely vegetarian. Rice is the staple food, and it is certainly possible to eat plain rice morning, noon, and night, but such a diet would be singularly unsatisfying. Unfortunately, the available accompaniments are often not suitable for strict vegetarians. Curries are very common, but usually contain meat of some kind. (Water-buffalo curry, anyone?) Most vegetable dishes and vegetable soups contain fish sauce (*nam pla*), dried shrimp, or both, and these seafood products are not always readily discernible. However, as one might expect, pesco-vegetarians should be able to eat well anywhere in the country. Noodles and salads are sometimes meat-free and fish-free.

There are very few specialty vegetarian restaurants, but there are a growing number of "health food" restaurants that serve low-fat, high-fiber foods which are meat-free. Chinese restaurants are also fairly common, and some serve vegetarian entrees. In the cities, many different Asian and Western cuisines are available. Restaurants that cater to Western travelers can be found in Bangkok, Chiang Mai, Phuket, and many other popular destinations. These restaurants generally serve vegetarian dishes.

Thai is the official language. Chinese dialects, Malay (Bahasa Indonesia) (p. 227), and a host of other minority languages and dialects are also spoken.

Thai

Thai employs a unique system of writing. The words and phrases below have been transliterated into the Roman alphabet. Thai is also a difficult tonal language. See the Note on Tonal Languages (p. 6) in the Introduction for a description of the symbols used below.

I would like something without _____. *(male speaker)*	Pohm khaw a'arai thii mii____.	⬈pohm ⬈kaw ah-rye ⬊tee mee ____
I would like something without ____. *(female speaker)*	Diichan khaw a'rai thii mii____.	dee ⬊chuhn ⬈kaw ah-rye ⬊tee mee ____
We would like something without ____.	Rau khaw a'rai thii mii ____.	rau ⬈kaw ah-rye ⬊tee mee ____
I do not eat ____. *(male speaker)*	Phom gin ____ mai dai gin.	⬈pohm keen ____ ⬊mye ⬊dye

I do not eat ____. *(female speaker)*	Diichan gin ____ mai dai gin.	dee ↗chuhn keen ____ ↘mye ↘dye
I eat ____. *(male speaker)*	Phom gin ____.	↗pohm keen ____
I eat ____. *(female speaker)*	Diichan gin ____.	dee ↗chuhn keen ____
meat	nya	↘neuah
chicken	gai	kye
fish	plaa	blah
fish sauce	nam plaa	nuhm blah
eggs	khai	kye
Thank you. *(male speaker)*	Khawp khun khrap.	kawp kuhn kruhp
Thank you. *(female speaker)*	Khawp khun kha.	kawp kuhn ↘kuh

Vietnam

As elsewhere in southeast Asia, rice is the staple food, and is eaten as part of virtually all meals; unfortunately, meat in some form usually accompanies the rice. The Vietnamese are particularly fond of pork, chicken, and fish. While the first two creatures are easy to spot, the fish fondness can pose problems; strict vegetarians face pitfalls at every turn, because fish sauce— *nuoc nam*—is added to all sorts of otherwise innocuous vegetable dishes. More esoteric animals, including endangered species, are also eaten from time to time; the ultimate vegetarian's horror is the "delicacy" of monkey brains— eaten directly out of the skull of a live, strapped-down monkey.

Despite the carnivorous habits of most Vietnamese, some occasionally indulge in periods of vegetarianism. Most cities have specialty vegetarian restaurants, as well as a small but rapidly increasing number of Western-style restaurants serving pizza and the like. Restaurants catering to Western travelers have opened in popular tourist centers; these usually offer at least one vegetarian entree. Outside of these areas, rice with vegetables is probably the best bet (but beware of fish sauce). Some restaurants may be willing to throw together something more elaborate for vegetarians.

Vietnamese is the official language. A variety of minority languages are spoken in more remote areas, especially along the borders with Cambodia and Laos. There is also a small Chinese-speaking minority.

Vietnamese

Vietnamese is a tonal language; see the Note on Tonal Languages (p. 6) in the Introduction for a description of the symbols used below.

I would like something without ____.	Tôi moốn món ăn không có ____.	doy↗moo-uhn↗mawn aan ahn kow↗ng koh ____
I do not eat ____.	Tôi không ăn ____.	doy kohmng aan ____
I eat ____ and ____.	Tôi ăn ____ và ____.	doy aan ____ ↘vah ____

Asia

meat	thịt	↗teet
chicken	thịt gà	↗teet ↘gah
fish	cá	↗kah
eggs	quả trứng	kwâh ↗choouhng
cheese	phó mát	↗faw ↗maht
Thank you. *(addressing a man)*	Cám ớn ông.	↗kamn uhn ohng
Thank you. *(addressing a woman)*	Cám ớn cô.	↗kahm uhn koh

chapter seven
AUSTRALIA AND THE PACIFIC

Although no person is an island, every country in this chapter is an island—a large island, a small island, or a group of islands. Being entirely surrounded by water, the peoples of these countries predictably consume a good deal of fish so pesco-vegetarians should be content anywhere. Traditionally, the peoples of the Pacific island nations have eaten lots of starches—yams, taro, cassava, other root vegetables, rice, and breadfruit—supplemented by coconuts, tropical fruit, greens, and of course fish. In the last half-century, however, these traditional diets have been corrupted by the influence of American and Australian junk food culture. In some areas, it is difficult to find traditional food, even in private homes. (Most Australians and New Zealanders, of course, have long had stereotypically "Western" diets.) On the other hand, it may be difficult to find anything other than starches, fish, and fruit on remote and undeveloped islands.

In large towns and in areas where tourists congregate, the culinary offerings may be more diverse: Chinese, Japanese, or even Indian restaurants can be found. In any case, it should not be a problem anywhere in the region to find something meatless on which to subsist (although choices may be very limited). Prospective visitors should not let dietary concerns delay their trip for too long; it is predicted that the most low-lying atolls may be engulfed by rising sea levels sometime in the next century.

Language
A range of Polynesian, Melanesian, Papuan, and aboriginal languages are spoken in this region. Many of these languages are only spoken by a few hundred people or even fewer, and are rapidly approaching extinction. Due to patterns of colonization English works perfectly well as a mode of communication in most countries of the Pacific, except on the French islands.

Because there is no indigenous dairy tradition in the Pacific, few of the languages listed below have a word for cheese. Generally, the English word "cheese" (or "fromage" in French-speaking areas) is used.

Australia
The convicts who were transported to Australia in the eighteenth and nineteenth centuries are not remembered in history books as gentle vegetarians. Therefore, it should come as no surprise to find that most of their descendants are ardent carnivores. Steak, lamb, or seafood (or some permutation thereof) is the centerpeice of an average Australian meal. This is especially the case in many small outback towns, where a vegetarian visitor may feel freakish and uncomfortable (although a healthy zest for beer can ameliorate local resentment). Travelers must also navigate around well-intentioned offers of such esoteric items as crocodile or kangaroo meat.

Fortunately, in the cities of Australia, there should be minimal problems in finding a vegetarian meal. Most large towns have at least one vegetarian or health food restaurant, and many ordinary restaurants are beginning to feature vegetarian entrees. There are also large Asian and European immigrant communities in the cities, particularly in Sydney, so ethnic eateries will usually be an option. Meatless meals are also realtively easy to find in the wine-producing regions of Victoria, Western Australia, and South Australia. Pesco-vegetarians will have an easy time, and will be close to ecstasy anywhere along Australia's coastline.

English is the principal language, and is spoken throughout Australia. Indigenous aboriginal languages are spoken in some areas of the outback, while Asian and European languages are used by immigrants to Australia.

Australia administers several overseas territories in the Indian and Pacific Oceans. The most significant of these is **Norfolk Island,** whose inhabitants grow tasty tropical fruit and speak English.

Fiji

Fijian food is somewhat more varied than the cuisine of many other Pacific nations because the population is ethnically split. Indigenous Fijians, who are of Melanesian-Polynesian origin, and Indians, who arrived as laborers in the nineteenth century, each make up close to half the nation's population. Ethnic Fijians traditionally have eaten standard Pacific Island food: breadfruit, rice, taro, cassava, fish, and assorted vegetables and greens. Fijian Indians are more amenable to vegetarianism; at Indian restaurants, rice with *daal* (lentils) is common, as are curries. Everyone partakes of the excellent tropical fruit in season. However, Western-style food has made considerable inroads, and American-and Australian-type fast-food is very common. European, Chinese, and other Asian cuisines are also available in the towns.

English is the official language. **Fijian** is used by ethnic Fijians, who generally can also speak English. Many Fijians of Indian descent speak Hindi (p. 191) or other Indian languages.

Fijian

I do not eat _____.	Au sega ni kana ____.	ow SAYNG-ah nee KAH-nah ____
meat	lewe-ni-manumanu	LAY-way nee mah-noo-MAH-noo
chicken	toa	toh-wah
fish	ika	EE-kah
eggs	yaloka	yah-LOH-kah
Thank you.	Vinaka vakalevu.	vee-NAH-kah vah-kah-LAY-voo

The French Islands

The French still possess an array of islands in the South Pacific, which they use for benign activities such as vacationing and, until recently, testing nuclear weapons. On all of these islands, **French** (p. 60) is an official (if not always the preferred) language.

New Caledonia, which in turn has its own dependencies, features an international culinary atmosphere. French restaurants and bakeries dot the lush landscape. Other Western-style restaurants, such as pizzerias, are very common. Indian, Southeast Asian, and Chinese restaurants complete the picture. Many locals eat traditional Pacific Island fare: taro, manioc, and banana dishes are all common (although hard to find in restaurants).

The overseas territory of **French Polynesia** comprises several archipelagic groups. Tahiti is the most well-known island.

Excellent French restaurants and bakeries exist here, but a whole host of international offerings is also available. Chinese, Indian, Italian, and even Middle Eastern restaurants can be found. Pesco-vegetarians will find amazing seafood. On Tahiti itself, indigenous food is surprisingly hard to find (although excellent tropical fruit is always available). However, on the outer islands, standard Pacific Island food such as fish and taro is typically consumed. Most islanders speak Tahitian as a first langauge, but they are perfectly competent in French.

The far-flung islands of **Wallis and Futuna** are little visited, and the local cuisine is comprised of Pacific Island standards such as coconuts, yams, taro root, and bananas.

Kiribati

This nation of low-lying island groups has an intimate relationship with the sea, and fish figures prominently in Kiribatian diets. Vegetarians who would like their relationship with the sea not to involve eating its denizens may choose from the standard array of Pacific island produce: taro, breadfruit, sweet potatoes, and assorted vegetables are grown on most inhabited islands where the soil is good enough. Rice is a common staple. Many basic foodstuffs are imported. On some islands, there are a few hotels and small restaurants that serve American-style food.

English is the official language. Most people use one of several indigenous Pacific languages at home.

Marshall Islands

Although astoundingly beautiful, the Marshalls are low-lying islands with poor soil. As a result, there are few vegetables and relatively little fruit. Apart from breadfruit and rice—and of course fish—the diet is highly Westernized, with a disappointing amount of American fast-food. A few restaurants offer more thoughtful versions of European-style food (and meatless dishes are usually available there). Otherwise, the Chinese and Japanese restaurants in the large towns are generally the best (although not a perfect) option for meat-free eating.

Marshallese is the national language, although **English** has official status and most islanders can speak it as a second language.

Marshallese

I do not eat _____.	Ijjab konnan mona ____.	EE-jahb koh-nahn moh-nah ____
meat	kaniok	kahn-yohk
chicken	bao	bah-oh
fish	iik	eek
eggs	lib	leeb
Thank you.	Kommol.	kohm-mohl

Micronesia

The Federated States of Micronesia occupy a large chunk of the western Pacific. What food is available depends to a large extent on where you are. In towns, fast-food, junk food, and Chinese and American restaurants rule the roost. In more isolated areas, traditional food such as rice, breadfruit, taro, and yams (and of course fish) is easier to find. Unfortunately, junk food is gaining supremacy even in fairly far-flung areas. Hotel and resort restaurants sometimes offer more imaginative dishes, and vegetarian food is often available (especially with advance notice).

English is the official language. Various Micronesian and Polynesian languages are spoken by Micronesians at home.

Nauru

Nauru's one and only product is phosphate. Despite being

essentially a mountain of fertilizer, Nauru must import virtually all of its food and most of its fresh water. Needless to say, fresh vegetables are far from plentiful, and food choice is generally restricted to rice or Western-style fast-food; there are also a few Chinese restaurants.

Nauruan is the official language, but most Nauruans can speak **English**, which is widely used in commerce and government.

New Zealand

In a country with several times more sheep than people, some of those sheep are bound to be devoured. One might expect New Zealand's cuisine to consist of nothing more than lamb and mutton. However, vegetarianism is surprisingly easy to manage here, even in small communities. The cities and some smaller towns have specialty vegetarian restaurants; in large communities, most standard restaurants offer one or two meatless entrees. (Vegans may have a problem, however, as vegetarian entrees usually contain cheese.) There are also Asian restaurants in the cities, which are more likely to offer vegetarian entrees than their counterparts in Asia. In rural areas, restaurants may not offer meatless dishes; this is not the case in wine-growing areas, where most restaurants will cater to vegetarians. Where restaurants fail, vegetarians will have no problem cooking for themselves as bulk food or natural food stores exist even in small towns.

English is New Zealand's official language. The indigenous Maori speak their own Polynesian language, but usually can also speak English.

The **Cook Islands, Tokelau,** and **Niue** are self-governing territories of New Zealand. Their food is generally the Polynesian trio of tubers, fruit, and fish, but more touristed areas offer more variety and it may even be impossible to get local food. Rarotonga, for example, has many good Western-style restaurants, although not all offer vegetarian entrees. English and Polynesian languages are spoken.

Palau

Palau is a small country of small islands, few people, and limited culinary options. Local cuisine is mostly based on rice, cassava, sweet potatoes, coconuts, and fish. In the towns, there are some Japanese and Chinese restaurants as well as western-style fast food. Vegetarian entrees are not commonly offered in the few hotel restaurants.

Both Palauan and **English** are official languages. Other indigenous languages are also spoken.

Papua New Guinea

To make the point that Papua New Guinea is not a vegetarian paradise, it should be mentioned that one isolated tribe eats the brains of its dead as a sign of respect (and contracts a malady related to mad cow disease as a result). It is true that you are unlikely to be invited to take part in this practice, but other perils await. Strange forest animals are often eaten in the interior. Less mobile and more traditional cuisine includes sweet potato, taro, sago palm, yam, bananas, and rice. This assortment is probably acceptable to many vegetarians, but is difficult to find. Most towns offer only Western-style hamburger joints or Chinese restaurants. (The latter are obviously a better bet for vegetarians.) Port Moresby has a wider variety of eateries, and more sophisticated Western-type food (such as pasta) and Asian cuisines are available. Pesco-vegetarians will find that fish is a staple along the coast and on the outer islands.

There are literally hundreds of Melanesian and Papuan languages spoken in Papua New Guinea. Although **English** is the official language, not everyone speaks it, particularly in the interior. The main medium of inter-group communication, even in fairly remote areas, is **Pidgin**. It should be obvious that Pidgin is derived from English, although most tourists will not be able to understand it.

Pidgin

I would like something without ____.	Mi laik kaikai i no gat ____.	mee lyke kye-kye ee noh gaht ____
I do not eat ____.	Mi no save kaikai ____.	mee noh sah-vay kye-kye ____
meat	mit	meet
chicken	kokaruk	koh-kah-rook
fish	pis	pees
eggs	kiau	kee-ow
Thank you.	Tenku tru.	tehn-kyoo troo

Solomon Islands

Traditional Solomon Islands cuisine is a basic diet of rice, fish, fruit, coconut, beans, and the usual Pacific starches: breadfruit, taro, yam, and sweet potato. Vegetarians can generally find something to eat from this assortment. In towns, Western and Chinese restaurants purvey the usual offerings. Hotel and resort restaurants occasionally serve vegetarian entrees. Tropical fruit here is widely available and generally outstanding. Chewing betel nut is a common habit in the Solomons. Since betel acts as an appetite suppressant, this could be a useful last resort if the available food offerings prove unsatisfactory.

English is the official language. Most inhabitants speak a Melanesian, Papuan, or Polynesian tongue as their first language.

Speaking Vegetarian

Pijin can be very useful in parts of the Solomons, and it is often used to bridge local linguistic barriers. Pijin is very similar to Papuan Pidgin, although there are a few differences in usage.

Pijin

I do not eat _____.	Mi no save kaikai _____.	mee noh sah-vay kye-kye _____
meat	mit	meet
chicken	kokorako	koh-koh-rah-koh
fish	fishi	fee-shee
eggs	egg	ehg
Thank you.	Taggio tumas.	tah-gyoh too-muhs

Tonga

Traditional Tongan food includes the usual suspects: fish, taro, yams, coconut, breadfruit, bananas and other tropical fruit, pork, and rice. Unfortunately, most restaurants do not serve traditional cuisine. Some "traditional" feasts, which are usually targeted at tourists, offer a selection of traditional foods; unfortunately, vegetarians are unlikely to find them particularly attractive, as the centerpiece is usually an imposing array of roast suckling pigs. Western-style restaurants are very common in towns, and sometimes do offer vegetarian entrees (although they are more likely to serve fish, chicken, or pork). Chinese and other Asian cuisines are also available.

Both **Tongan** and **English** are official languages.

Tongan

I do not eat _____.	'Oku 'ikai teu kai _____.	OH-koo EE-kye tay-oo kye _____
meat	kakano'i manu	kah-kah-noh-ee MAH-noo
chicken	moa	moh-wah
fish	ika	EE-kah
eggs	fo'i moa	foh-ee moh-wah
cheese	siisi	see-see
Thank you.	Malō.	MAH-loh

Tuvalu

Tuvalu is only 9 square miles of coral atolls, which have generally poor soil, so most foodstuffs must be imported. As one would expect, variety and freshness are not the watchwords of Tuvaluan food, and processed junk food is the order of the day (with some very limited exceptions, such as breadfruit). You should have no difficulty finding coconut, at any rate; it is the main export commodity.

Tuvaluan and **English** are the main languages.

The U.S. Islands

Guam is the most developed of the U.S. Pacific possessions (and of all mid-Pacific islands generally). Guam is "where America's day begins," but that doesn't mean vegetarians are guaranteed a decent breakfast. American restaurant chains are well-represented; there are also many independent restaurants, some of which serve interesting meatless dishes. About a quarter of Guam's population was born in Asia, so Chinese, Japanese, Filipino, and other Asian cuisines are easily available. Guam produces plenty of vegetables and local markets are good places to enjoy a respite from processed food.

The **Northern Marianas** Islands, stretching north from Guam, are somewhat more traditional and less cosmopolitan than Guam (with the exception of Saipan, which is quite developed).

In both Guam and the Northern Marianas, **English** is treated as the official language, although many islanders speak Chamorro at home.

In **American Samoa**, the traditional fare is like that of Western Samoa—fish, taro, breadfruit, yams, bananas, and coconuts are the main staples. However, Western-style restaurants (and dreadful fast-food outlets) from the United States are beginning to establish culinary hegemony; it may be difficult to find traditional Samoan food. Most people in American Samoa are bilingual in **Samoan** (p. 253) and **English**.

Assorted other insular American possessions are scattered around the Pacific; most are uninhabited or are used for military purposes, and the authorities are unlikely to welcome visitors—vegetarian or otherwise—blundering around.

Vanuatu

Vanuatu offers the usual Pacific island staples of taro, breadfruit, coconut, cassava, and the like. These islands are heavily forested and an excellent selection of tropical fruits is available. There are also plenty of Western-type cafes and restaurants in the towns, as well as a selection of Chinese restaurants.

English and **French** (p. 60) are both official languages, but various Melanesian languages are spoken in Vanuatuan homes. The most common medium of inter-group communication is Bislama, which is very close to **Pijin** and **Pidgin**; those dialects can usually be understood in Bislama's stead.

Western Samoa

Western Samoa has fertile soil and an excellent climate, resulting in an enticing range of local produce. Traditionally, Samoans consume plenty of root vegetables—especially taro root, which is sometimes served with a sauce of coconut cream. Taro leaves are used in traditional dishes. Breadfruit is another starchy staple, and bananas (sometimes cooked and served as a side dish) and other tropical fruit are easily available. However, it is sometimes difficult to find traditional food outside Samoan homes or touristy feasts (beware the obligatory roast suckling pig at the latter). Restaurants and fast-food joints tend to focus on Western fast-food and Chinese dishes, although curries and other interesting meatless possibilities can also be found. Pesco-vegetarians will be happy to learn that fish is exceedingly common.

Both **Samoan** and **English** are official languages. Most Samoans are bilingual, although few people speak English in very remote areas, especially on Savaii.

Samoan

I do not eat _____. *(polite usage)*	Ou te le taumafa i le _____.	oo tay lay tow-MAH-fah ee lay _____
I do not eat _____. *(colloquial usage)*	Ou te le ai i le _____.	oo tay lay eye ee lay _____
meat *(generally refers only to beef)*	fasi povi	FAH-see POH-vee
pork	fasi pua'a	FAH-see poo-AH-ah

chicken	fasi moa	FAH-see moh-wah
fish	ia	ee-ah
eggs	fua moa	foo-ah moh-wah
cheese	sisi	see-see
I am a vegetarian. *(literally, "I do not eat the flesh of animals")*	Ou te le ai i aano o manu.	oo tay lay eye ee ah-ah-noh oh MAH-noo
Thank you.	Faafetai.	fah-ah-feh-tye

INDEX OF LANGUAGES

INDEX OF COUNTRIES AND TERRITORIES